Saltwater Aquarium

Handbook

George Blasiola

With Full-color Photographs
Drawings by Michele Earle-Bridges

BARRON'S

Dedication

For my parents, who supported my early scientific collecting forays, fishy endeavors, and menagerie of animals, from sea horses and iguanas to flying squirrels.

About the Author

George Blasiola, Marine Biologist B.S., M.A., is an internationally known specialist in marine fish biology, especially in the area of marine fish diseases. He was formerly associated with the Steinhart Aquarium, California Academy of Sciences, San Francisco. Mr. Blasiola was the Director of Research and Development for the Wardley Corporation. As chief scientist, he led an expedition to the Philippines in 1986 to investigate the effects of destructive fishing on coral reefs. Currently, he is the owner/consultant for Aqua-Sphere Research. He is the author of over 100 articles in scientific journals and popular magazines and has lectured worldwide. He is a contributing editor to *Freshwater and Marine Aquarium* magazine and a consultant and contributing editor to *Pet Age* magazine.

Photo Credits

Aaron Norman: pages 2, 7, 11, 21, 36, 43, 46, 58, 71, 77, 82, 88, 94, 99, 105, 113, 114, 130, 143, 152, 158; Zig Leszczynski: pages 8, 24, 100, 108, 124, 155.

Cover Photos

Aaron Norman

All inquiries should be addressed to:
Barron's Educational Series, Inc.
250 Wireless Boulevard
Hauppauge, New York 11788
http://www.barronseduc.com

Library of Congress Catalog Card No. 99-26660

International Standard Book No. 0-7641-1241-4

Library of Congress Cataloging-in-Publication Data
Blasiola, George C.
    The saltwater aquarium handbook / George Blasiola ; with color photographs by Aaron Norman and drawings by Michele Earle-Bridges ; consulting editor, Matthew M. Vriends. – [Rev. ed.].
    p. cm.
Rev. ed. of: The new saltwater aquarium handbook. 1991.
    Includes bibliographical references and index.
    ISBN 0-7641-1241-4 (pb)
    1. Marine aquariums Handbooks, manuals, etc.
I. Vriends, Matthew M., 1937– . II. Title.
SF457.1.B58   2000
639.34'2—dc21   99-26660
                                            CIP

Printed in Hong Kong

987654

Important Note

In this book, electrical equipment for the maintenance of aquariums is described. Please be sure to observe the manufacturer's instructions; otherwise serious accidents may occur. Before buying a large aquarium, check how much weight the floor can support in the location where you will set up the aquarium.

It is not always possible to avoid water damage resulting from broken glass, overflow, or leaks that develop in the tank; therefore, be sure to obtain insurance against such accidents. This can generally be part of your homeowners or other liability policy. Also, be sure to keep all fish medications, disinfectants, and other chemicals out of reach of children.

Contents

Introduction   1
    Acknowledgments   2

1. The Marine Aquarium   3
    Types of Aquariums   4
    Size of the Aquarium   5
    Tank Shape   6
    Aquarium Weight and Placement   8

2. Marine Aquarium Equipment   9
    Aquarium Filtration   9
    Protein Skimmers   11
    Use of Ozone Generators and Ultraviolet Sterilizers   12
    Major Types of Filter Equipment   13
    Filter Materials   17
    Other Aquarium Accessories   19
    Lighting Requirements   22

3. Water and Water Quality   25
    Natural Seawater   25
    Synthetic Seawater   26
    Water Parameters   27
    Nitrogen Compounds   30
    Phosphate   32

4. Setting Up the Aquarium   33
    Tank Location   33
    Substrate   33
    Conditioning Water   35
    Decorating Your Aquarium   35
    Algae in the Marine Aquarium   39
    Procedure for Setting Up the Aquarium   43

5. Selecting Marine Fish   47
    Carrying Capacity of Aquariums   47

Purchasing Fish for the Aquarium 48
Introducing New Fish into Your Aquarium 49
The Acclimation Period—The First Few Weeks 50
Community Aquariums 50
Maintaining Fish Compatibility 51
A Survey of Aquarium Fish 52

6. Selecting Marine Invertebrates 83
Purchasing Invertebrates for the Aquarium 84
Acclimating New Invertebrates 84
Aquariums with Fish and Invertebrates 84
A Survey of Marine Invertebrates 85

7. The Aquarium Conditioning Period 101
The Nitrogen Cycle 102
Conditioning Your New Aquarium 103
Monitoring the Aquarium 106
After the Conditioning Period 107

8. Aquarium Maintenance 109
Keeping a Journal 109
Daily Maintenance 110
Weekly and Monthly Maintenance 112

9. Nutrition 119
Marine Fish Nutrition 119
Feeding Behavior of Marine Fish 120
Dietary Requirements: A Brief Survey 121
Types of Foods for Marine Fish and Invertebrates 125
Guidelines for Feeding Marine Fish 131
Guidelines for Feeding Marine Invertebrates 133
Feeding Aquatic Animals While You Are Away 134

10. Diseases of Marine Fish 135
The Stress Response 136
Disease Recognition and Prevention 136
Quarantining Aquarium Fish 139
Common Diseases of Marine Fish 144

Appendices 159

Useful Addresses and Literature 160

Index 161

Introduction

Watching an aquarium full of fish and invertebrates is an enjoyable and relaxing pastime. The marine aquarium hobby still continues to attract large numbers of people who wish to enjoy a part of nature in their home. With such a large body of knowledge and reliable equipment available, you can set up and maintain a marine aquarium just as easily as a freshwater one. Since the original edition of this book, new advances in the area of fish care, disease prevention, and nutrition have helped unravel many of the problematic areas that affect the success of aquarium keeping. As with all things, a prerequisite to success is a basic understanding of the principles of keeping a saltwater aquarium. It is those basic fundamentals that are often overlooked but that are the keystone to success.

The majority of marine organisms still sold for aquariums are captured in the wild and are therefore removed from their natural habitat, although, in the past eight years, a large number of marine fish have successfully been bred. Unfortunately, a large number of these fish are not always found in the industry, so we still rely on capturing fish. It is my viewpoint that keeping coral reef fish and invertebrates in captivity requires the hobbyist to assume responsible custodianship. This responsibility extends to understanding and fulfilling the special requirements for providing coral reef animals with a healthy environment, and it also means that success must truly be measured not by how many different fish one can keep, but rather by their longevity due to proper care.

The Saltwater Aquarium Handbook, Second Edition, introduces the beginner to the fundamentals of the marine hobby, which has undergone rapid expansion since the early 1960s. In this edition, all the major critical topics are covered, including proper equipment selection, how to purchase healthy animals, how to choose from a guide to recommended fish and invertebrates, maintenance of the aquarium, nutrition, and common health problems of fish. Many sections have been expanded to include new information on protein skimmers, trickle filters, coral care in aquariums, and feeding fish properly.

▲ *Left: The Copperband Butterflyfish* (Chelmon rostratus). *Right: The Pijama Cardinalfish* (Sphaeramia nematoptera).

A thorough understanding of the basic information in this handbook will prepare you to establish and maintain in your home or workplace a small but flourishing replicate of the ocean realm.

Acknowledgments

Special appreciation is due to the following individuals who were helpful in both the original and revised editions of this book: Matthew M. Vriends, for guidance throughout the first edition project; Marty Kendrik, for his assistance in providing supplemental information on aquarium fish; Aaron Norman, for his review of the manuscript and useful remarks and suggestions, as well as his excellent photographs; Michelle Earle-Bridges, for her exceptional work on the illustrations; and the Barron's staff, who always make these projects an enjoyable and rewarding experience.

Chapter One

The Marine Aquarium

It's not hard not to be captivated when watching the brilliant colors, bizarre shapes, and graceful movements of fishes and invertebrates from a coral reef. And, while viewing these creatures at a public aquarium or while snorkeling in some part of the world, few of us have not imagined, at least for a moment, having a small piece of this undersea world in our home or office.

In contrast to aquariums for freshwater tropical fish or goldfish, marine aquariums follow a different set of requirements. Although there are many similarities, there are enough notable differences to warrant a more in-depth understanding of the requirements of the marine environment and the sea creatures themselves before setting up your first marine aquarium. However, despite what you may have heard about the difficulties of maintaining such aquariums, they are easier to maintain than ever. Keeping healthy, beautiful coral reef fish and invertebrates is no longer an impossibility. With the great popularity of the hobby, it is possible to purchase marine animals that have been col-

lected from all over the world—including Fiji, the Philippines, Hawaii, the Caribbean, and the Red Sea.

Three decades ago, obtaining and successfully keeping marine fish and invertebrates was quite difficult, often impossible, for most people. Little information was available on the specific requirements of the fish and invertebrates. The knowledge needed to properly filter the water, avoid water pollution, provide sound diets, and control disease was lacking. With the advent of more sophisticated equipment, synthetic salt mixes, commercial diet mixtures, improved testing equipment, and better handling of fish, almost anyone can start and maintain a healthy functioning marine aquarium. However, even with state-of-the-art equipment, success will not be achieved without a thorough understanding of the fundamentals of care and management.

The first few chapters in this book cover the selection of the required equipment for an aquarium. This is followed by a discussion of filtration and water quality. The discussions are geared to the first-time marine

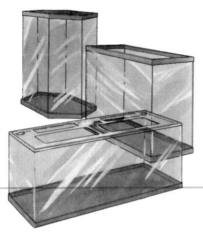

Aquariums are made in various shapes and sizes to fit easily in any area of a home or office. All-glass or acrylic aquariums are readily available.

aquarium hobbyist and present the basic principles for setting up and maintaining a successful aquarium.

Types of Aquariums

An aquarium is a container that houses aquatic life, whereas a terrarium is a container that houses land plants and animals. Aquariums are also referred to as "fish tanks."

A wide variety of commercially available aquariums are designed specifically for marine organisms. The large number of styles, shapes, and sizes will fit just about everyone's taste. Designs include freestanding rectangular, spherical (fish-eye), and square tanks—as well as models that resemble a low coffee table. Some

manufacturers will custom-build an aquarium to fill a buyer's design request.

Regardless of shape, the two basic materials used in construction are glass and acrylic. There are advantages and disadvantages to each type.

All-Glass Aquariums

The most readily available types of glass tanks are constructed entirely of glass. Capacity varies from 10 gallons (37.8 L) to hundreds of gallons. All glass tanks are constructed of plate glass, held together by a non-toxic silicone adhesive. The thickness of the glass increases substantially as the size of the tank increases. The entire tank is then framed with plastic moldings for a finished appearance. The moldings vary; many are finished in either black or a simulated wood grain. Depending on the manufacturer, the upper molding might include an inside rim, which allows support for a cover glass to minimize evaporation.

All glass tanks may be used for either saltwater or freshwater fish. Never use an aquarium that is constructed of any type of metal—not even stainless steel, which was once widely used in aquariums. Salt water will readily corrode metals. The metal salts formed are highly toxic to marine fish and invertebrates. All-glass aquariums are readily available, long-lasting, and they contain no toxic materials. The only disadvantage is that larger-sized aquariums are very heavy because of the increased glass thickness required to withstand water pressure.

Small all-glass tanks can be constructed using five precut panes of high-strength glass and silicone adhesive. This is not recommended, however, because poorly constructed tanks will not hold water or, if scaled improperly, can develop leaks. With the ready availability of all-glass tanks, it makes little sense to construct one. In addition, quality manufacturers will guarantee their products from leaking.

When you select your aquarium, inspect all parts to ensure that there are no cracks in any of the glass panes. Closely inspect the inside seams to ensure that there is a continuous seal of silicone cement. An irregular seal of cement along the seams eventually could cause leaks.

Acrylic Aquariums

Acrylic plastics are quite strong and can be molded into various shapes. The acrylic pieces that form such tanks are joined with a solvent bonding cement. Many of these aquariums feature curved front corners that make a beautiful showpiece. Acrylic aquariums are available in various sizes and shapes, most commonly rectangular, square, or hexagonal.

The advantages of acrylic are that it is relatively lightweight, crack resistant, and it permits better front viewing of the fish and invertebrates because of the tank's curved front corners, but it tends to be more expensive than glass. Acrylic can easily be scratched by cleaning objects or pieces of gravel—a minor disadvantage. An aquarist who is careful while cleaning the aquarium will seldom cause serious damage. If scratches do occur, however, special scratch removers are available to refinish the damaged area. (If the inside of the aquarium is scratched, the entire tank will need to be drained to make the repairs.)

Size of the Aquarium

Determining the proper size of the aquarium depends on the number and type of fish, the available space, and economic constraints. To the new marine hobbyist the best advice is, the larger the aquarium, the better.

Marine aquariums must be larger than their freshwater counterparts. Whereas a 10-gallon (37.8 L) tank can be perfectly suitable for freshwater tropical fish or goldfish, the same size can cause major problems when maintaining marine fish. Many species of marine fish are very territorial and require large areas to coexist peacefully with other species. Also, smaller aquariums may foul rapidly, so once a problem occurs you have little time to correct the situation. Therefore, the larger the aquarium, the better.

As a general rule, start with a standard rectangular aquarium with a capacity of 20 to 40 gallons (75.6 to 151.4 L). The approximate dimensions of a 20-gallon "show-type aquarium" are 30 × 12 × 12 inches (76 × 30 × 30 cm). The same volume aquarium is also available with dimensions of 24 × 12 × 16 inches (61 × 30 × 41 cm). Both types are suitable; however, the longer and shallower show type is particularly good for community aquariums with fish and invertebrates. As will be discussed in a later chapter, these tanks are also more suitable for growing seaweeds (macroalgae).

It is not impossible to maintain marine fish in smaller quarters, but that should be avoided for several reasons. If a problem develops, it can result in the death of the fish long before you can discover and correct the situation. For example, with a power failure, the temperature will change rapidly in a small 10-gallon (37.8-L) aquarium. As will be discussed later, water quality deterioration due to the buildup of wastes also occurs much more rapidly in a small aquarium.

In summary, the size of the tank is not where a marine hobbyist should economize. Select the largest one that you can accommodate and afford.

Tank Shape

You also should give careful consideration to the shape of your aquarium. The various available shapes have a direct effect on the watery environment. Long tanks provide greater surface area and reduced depth. High tanks provide greater depth and reduced surface area. The greater the surface area of the tank, the better the gas exchange at the water surface—and therefore the more rapid the dissipation of carbon dioxide and the absorption of oxygen. Certain aquarium shapes can appear pleasing to the eye, but may not have the environmental advantages offered by more standard designs. For example, fish-eye tanks provide an ultramodern appearance, but are generally unsuitable because of an extreme reduction in surface area. The number of animals that can be maintained in such tanks is quite limited. In addition, maintenance of fish-eye aquariums is often very difficult and time-consuming, including the cleaning of the gravel, addition and removal of decorative items and fish, and simple cleaning of the inside surfaces.

As a general rule, if two aquariums of the same volume differ in the size of their surfaces, select the one that provides the greater surface area.

Aquarium Weight and Placement

A very important consideration in deciding the size of the aquarium is its total weight when in full operation. In determining where the aquarium is to be placed, you must consider the combined weight of the

▲ *Left: The Pinnatus Batfish* (Platax pinnatus) *is readily sought after for aquariums. Right: The Ornate Butterflyfish* (Chaetodon ornatissimus), *although beautiful, should not be purchased due to its poor survival record in aquariums.*

aquarium, water, decorations, coral rock, and so on.

An aquarium can be placed on a piece of furniture if it is capable of supporting the weight. Keep in mind that salt water eventually will get on the furniture. It is therefore recommended that you purchase a cabinet or stand specifically designed to support an aquarium. Numerous styles of wood or wood-grain finish cabinets are sold, often with storage space for air pumps, filters, and

other equipment. Other cabinets or stands provide space for an additional small aquarium.

You also must be certain that the floor in your home will support the weight of an aquarium. If you live on the upper floor of an apartment or condominium, check to determine what weight can be supported. This is especially important in older buildings. There is no need for such concern for smaller tanks; only larger tanks could pose a problem. For example, a 200-gallon (756-L) aquarium filled with water (without the weight of the aquarium, gravel, or anything else) weighs approximately 1,700 pounds (771 kg). When added together, the total weight would well exceed a ton!

Chapter Two
Marine Aquarium Equipment

The basic equipment for a marine aquarium is similar to equipment needed for a freshwater aquarium. The most important pieces of equipment are the filters, responsible for the purification of the aquarium water. Various types of filtration equipment are available, each performing single or multiple functions. Some filter equipment is optional, while others are an absolute necessity for purifying the aquarium water.

Aquarium Filtration

The purpose of filtration in a marine aquarium is to maintain water quality to sustain the life of the inhabitants. Marine fish and invertebrates are far more sensitive to water quality deterioration than freshwater fish and invertebrates.

The process of filtration is divided into three types—biological, mechanical, and chemical. A properly selected and fully functional filter system will be able to perform all three types of filtration in a marine aquarium.

◄ *The Fairy Basslet or Purple Queen* (Mirolabrichthys tuka).

Biological filtration detoxifies waste products that accumulate in the water as a result of the normal metabolic activities of the marine organisms. Mechanical filtration maintains a crystal clear aquarium by the removal of particulate matter. Improper removal of suspended particles results in a cloudy appearance of the aquarium water. Finally, chemical filtration through the use of certain chemical filtrants or filter devices will reduce dissolved organic compounds that constantly accumulate in the water.

Biological Filtration

Biological filtration is the process by which specific types of bacteria detoxify toxic nitrogen compounds in aquarium water to less harmful compounds. The process by which this occurs is known as nitrification (see page 103) and is primarily mediated by two major types (genera) of bacteria, *Nitrosomonas* and *Nitrobacter*.

Nitrosomonas bacteria utilize ammonia as their energy source and transform ammonia into a less toxic compound called nitrite. Ammonia is the principal waste product of fish and also enters the water through the decomposition of food and other nitrogen-containing compounds. Nitrite is then utilized by *Nitrobacter,* which transforms it to less toxic nitrate. The process goes further through a denitrification phase in which nitrate can be chemically converted to free nitrogen or nitrous oxide.

The cyclic process just described is known as the nitrogen cycle. It occurs in all aquarium systems and is the most important type of filtration.

The nitrifying bacteria that detoxify the toxic products in the water are primarily concentrated in the filter bed substrate, although they are present on all surfaces of the aquarium. In the filter bed, provided conditions are favorable to the bacteria, they will multiply rapidly. These bacteria are classified as aerobic, since they require the presence of dissolved oxygen in order to carry out their filter activities. In contrast, other types of bacteria termed anaerobic decompose organic materials without the presence of oxygen. However, their activities produce substances such as hydrogen sulfide and methane that are toxic to aquatic life. The presence of a properly functioning and maintained filter system prevents the development of these anaerobic bacteria.

Mechanical Filtration

Mechanical filtration is the process by which particulate matter is removed from the water. Mechanical filtration is accomplished in the filter bed through outside filters that use foam inserts, filter floss, or other particulate matter trapping.

An undergravel filter, when set up and functioning properly, is a very efficient mechanical filter. The trapping of particulate matter occurs in the gravel bed as water flows through the substrate (gravel bed). However, if the undergravel filter is relied on as the only means of mechanical filtration, the filter bed can quickly become clogged as detritus accumulates. The use of supplementary filter media such as filter floss or foam in outside filters is therefore recommended to remove particulate matter from the aquarium water.

Chemical Filtration

Chemical filtration is the process by which dissolved organic compounds are removed from the water. Although organics are the primary materials removed by chemical filtration, other substances such as nitrogen compounds can also be removed this way.

This type of filtration uses specialized chemical filter media that are added to supplementary filters, other than an undergravel filter. Various types of media are available; the most common one used in marine aquariums is activated carbon. Chemical filtration can also be accomplished by using foam fractionation (use of protein skimmers) or ozone or ultraviolet irradiation.

The use of a protein skimmer can be very beneficial in aquariums with larger numbers of fish, but it is generally unnecessary in aquariums with a low density of fish. Ozone and ultraviolet irradiation equipment should also be considered optional. They are not required for the successful operation of a marine aquarium.

The accumulation of organic compounds originates from the metabolic activities of the aquatic animals. The accumulation of organics is often first noticed as the clear seawater in the aquarium begins to take on a yellowish cast. This color change is due to the presence of organics that continually concentrate themselves in the water if they are not removed through chemical filtration. The yellow color can make the aquarium look drab, but there are more serious problems associated with organic accumulation.

First, the accumulation of organics can interfere with the normal growth and development of fish and can be toxic to invertebrates. Larval fishes and various invertebrates such as delicate corals do poorly in water with high organic concentrations. Second, organics add to the amount of detritus that can clog filters. Also, increased detritus can initiate the increased multiplication of certain bacteria that add extra waste products to the aquarium water.

Protein Skimmers

Protein skimmers, or foam tractionators, have been around for a long time and have long been popular with European aquarists. Protein skimmers are an efficient means of removing dissolved organic materials from water. Since the buildup of organic materials can have an adverse effect on aquatic organisms, especially invertebrates, protein skimmers are an important piece of equipment for use in marine aquariums. They are capable of removing various types of organics including proteins, fatty acids, phosphate, colloids, and various other chemical substances. Organics containing metals such as copper or iron, as well as organics given off by invertebrates such as sea anemones and corals, are also removed by protein skimmers.

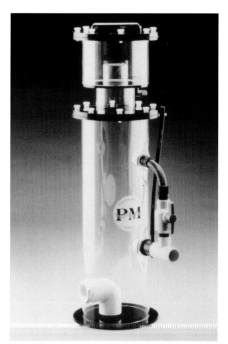

This protein skimmer requires minimum maintenance.

There are two main design types: co-current (unidirectional flow of air and water), counter-current (opposing flow). The counter-current design is recognized as a more efficient design, primarily because it permits a longer contact time with the bubbles in the reaction chamber. Protein skimmers using a counter-current design are the most common type available. These devices are available for internal mounting onto an aquarium or can be external as well. A third type of skimmer is known as a venturi protein skimmer. This utilizes a special device, a venturi valve, that introduces air under pressure into the filter. It is powered by an external pump.

Even though there are several designs for protein skimmers, the basic principle remains the same. As air is added to the reaction chamber, the small bubbles produced come into contact with dissolved organic materials. Contact time and bubble size are critical factors for the proper functioning of a protein skimmer. The air is produced from an air pump through diffusers or by a venturi action by pulling in atmospheric air using a venturi valve device. The bubbles carry the attached organics to the surface chamber where they form a foam, which continues to build until the volume of foam is forced into a dry collection chamber where it liquefies. The organics are disposed of once a sufficient amount has accumulated.

The disadvantage associated with skimmers is that they are able to remove trace elements required by fish and invertebrates. However, trace elements can easily be replenished by the regular addition of trace elements solutions or by more frequent water changes. The importance of water changes and their frequency will be discussed in Chapter 3 (page 25).

Protein skimmers require minimum maintenance; however, the collecting area for the foam should be inspected on a regular basis and the contents emptied. If you are using an air stone in the skimmer, you will need to inspect it for clogging by minerals.

Use of Ozone Generators and Ultraviolet Sterilizers

The use of ozone generators and ultraviolet sterilizers will effectively remove dissolved organics in marine aquarium water; it is also effective in destroying agents responsible for fish diseases.

Ozone Generators

Ozone-generating equipment, like protein skimmers, is also popular in Europe and more recently has aroused renewed interest on the part of American aquarists. Ozone generators are more useful in aquarium systems that house large numbers of fish and where there is a need to control the amount of rapidly accumulating dissolved organics and the concentration of microorganisms.

These units generate ozone, a form of oxygen that is in a highly energized form of three oxygen molecules, O_3. This form of oxygen is capable of oxidizing, or breaking down, various chemical compounds and destroying disease-causing microorganisms. The major disadvantage of ozone is that one must maintain a narrow acceptable concentration because of ozone's toxicity to fish and other aquatic organisms. Also, the amount of ozone in water is not easily measured or easily regulated, making it virtually impossible for an aquarist to know if the concentration in the aquarium water is approaching toxic levels. Therefore, ozone gas must never be added directly to water, but to a reacting chamber first before the treated water returns to the aquarium. Various small ozone generators are available commercially for marine aquariums.

With this in mind, ozone should be considered an option, especially for a person new to the marine hobby. Marine aquariums can operate well without ozone generators.

Ultraviolet Sterilizers

Ultraviolet sterilizers have been used for many years in larger aquariums, tropical fish holding facilities, and particularly in public aquariums. Ultraviolet sterilizers primarily control the concentration in the water of bacteria, viruses, and fungi, all potential causes of fish disease. Irradiation is best used in larger aquariums with large numbers of fish, in which the system can benefit by reducing the buildup of microorganisms.

Various types of units are available commercially. Since many factors play a role in the efficacy of this type of equipment, it is important to select the proper type of unit. One important criterion is the dosage of ultraviolet light that a UV unit emits during its operation. By convention, UV output is measured in microwatt seconds per square centimeter (u W/cm^2). Aquarium ultraviolet units should be able to provide a minimum of 35,000 u W/cm^2. This dosage rate is capable of killing bacteria, viruses, and other microbes. As with ozone generators, they should be considered as optional equipment for an aquarium.

Major Types of Filter Equipment

In order to purify your aquarium water, you will need to obtain filter equipment to perform biological, mechanical, and chemical filtration. Previously, I have discussed several optional types of chemical filters. The filters discussed in this section are required for a marine aquarium to maintain optimum water quality. There are numerous types and designs of commercial filters for aquariums. The basic types of filters fall into the following categories:

undergravel (subsand) filters, trickle filters, outside power filters, and canister filters.

The basic recommendation for a new marine hobbyist is to use an undergravel filter in combination with one of the other major types of filters discussed in this section.

Undergravel Filters

The undergravel filter is constructed of a raised perforated plate with hundreds of slits to permit a uniform flow of water through the filter bed. The slits are small enough to prevent substrate materials such as dolomite, crushed coral, or other media from falling through the plate. A series of tube openings allows the insertion of a tube assembly that contains a water lift, tubes, and an air line equipped with a diffuser. The air line is connected to an air pump that drives the filter.

The plates are placed on the aquarium bottom with a few inches of substrate placed on the filter top. The filter plates acts as a false bottom. While in operation, air is rapidly bubbled inside each lift tube. This action removes water from beneath the filter plate as the water exits the lift tube and causes aerating turbulence near the surface. This action creates a pull of water through the filter bed. The amount of water pulled through the bed is regulated by the flow rate from the air pump.

An alternative means to power filters is through the use of a power head. The unit attaches to the filter and increases the water flow rate through the filter bed. Some new designs also include easy adjustments for increasing or decreasing the flow rate. There are also indicators allowing the aquarist to check for any decrease in the initially set flow rate. This can indicate that the filter bed is becoming clogged and needs cleaning.

Undergravel filters function as both biological and mechanical filters. The undergravel filter was once considered basic equipment for the marine aquarist; however, these filters are not considered standard equipment now. The new basic equipment is more often a trickle filter, which will be discussed in the next section.

Undergravel filters do allow you to use any depth of gravel on the aquarium bottom without being concerned about the development of anaerobic bacteria in the filter bed. These bacteria, unlike nitrifying bacteria, develop in areas where little or no oxygen is available. The chemicals produced by these bacteria are highly toxic to marine fish and invertebrates. The presence of dark gray or black areas in the aquarium filter bed, accompanied by a rotten egg odor, indicates a malfunction of the filter bed and the development of anaerobic bacteria.

Undergravel filters are available in many shapes and sizes to fit almost any aquarium configuration. They are easily installed and require only an air pump or power head for operation.

Marine aquariums can function with only an undergravel filter, but an additional filter will ensure optimal water quality. Aquariums equipped with just an undergravel filter must maintain a low number of fish and require more frequent water changes. These filters have a tendency to produce high nitrates over time; therefore, they need frequent water changes when used by themselves. Since these filters do not perform chemical filtration, another type of filter will permit the use of activated carbon or other media to remove dissolved organics. A second filter also provides additional mechanical filtration, removing suspended particles.

In contrast to the undergravel filter, which is located in the aquarium, trickle filters, outside power filters, and canister filters are located externally. Numerous variations and styles of these filters are available, but all follow basic principles for water filtration.

Trickle Filters

The earliest filter that helped initiate the interest in reef-type aquariums in the United States was known as the wet/dry filter, a type of trickle filter. These filters became popular in the late 1980s. They were well known in Europe previous to their introduction to the United States market. The filter differs from others in that the filter media is not completely submerged in water; rather, it is kept moist by a continuous water spray or drip. The filter medium can vary from plastic wire or floss media to bioblocks, bioballs, or special synthetic material. The first wet/dry filters had a series of trays that used gravel as the filter media.

In trickle filters the bacteria are exposed to air and are able to utilize the oxygen required to maintain their metabolism. These devices maximize nitrification in one portion of the filter by the use of selected media that allow bacteria to proliferate; thus, the nitrification process is very efficient. This makes trickle filters an excellent filter for the first-time marine aquarist.

Some design modifications to this filter included a separate chamber where a small portion of water was in contact with anaerobic bacteria. The chamber was also supplied with a special organic food source. As a result, these denitrifier chambers allowed the conversion of nitrate to nitrite to nitrous oxide and then to free nitrogen. Depending on the quality of the design, some of these chambers can contribute to some denitrification, while others are virtually useless.

The trickle filter is the most popular filter today when starting a marine aquarium. There are various configurations and designs. The trickle filter uses media such as plastic bioblocks or rock. The filter water is distributed by spraying or through a drip plate, then the water flows evenly over the filter media, flows by gravity to a sump, and then is pumped back to the aquarium.

Outside Power Filters

Outside power filters are designed to hang on the back of the aquarium. They are powered with their own centrifugal pump, so an air pump is not required. Early models of the outside filter did require an air pump, but sophisticated technology has produced high-quality outside filters with their own power supply.

Interior design varies, but basically an outside filter is a vertical box with a series of compartments. The power source is usually located on the bottom of the filter. When in operation, a siphon draws water into the first compartment, from which it flows upward through a series of filter layers into another compartment. Depending on the filter design, there can be a series of separate compartments in the filter. The filter medium that can be placed in the filter compartments depends on the preference of the hobbyist. Most commonly, activated carbon or filter floss is used to perform chemical filtration and mechanical filtration. The filter medium is replaced every 4 to 12 weeks, depending on the number of fish in the aquarium and the type of filtrant in the filter chambers.

Canister Filters

Canister filters function essentially the same as outside power filters, but are freestanding. They too are self-powered, but with the pump on top of the filter. Most canister filters are considerably more expensive that other types of outside filters, especially if they are manufactured outside the United States. However, various domestic companies are producing less expensive canister filters that perform as well as more costly ones.

In contrast to filters that hang on the back of the aquarium, canister filters can be hidden in a cabinet beneath the aquarium, with only the intake and return lines visible in the aquarium.

When in operation, water flows by gravity to the canister intake at the bottom of the filter. The water flows upward through a series of filtrants (activated carbon, filter floss, and so on) that purify and clear the water, which is then pumped back into the aquarium. This versatile filter can use many layers of filter media, including activated carbon, foam filter pads, floss, calcareous materials for pH control, or other specialized filter media. The filter is also capable of performing biological filtration.

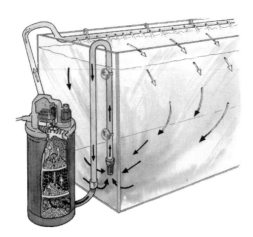

Canister filters are freestanding units that utilize various layers of filter media. They are hidden easily from view in cabinets located in many aquarium stands.

Foam or Sponge Filters

Foam or sponge filters are constructed of a porous foam cartridge that performs biological and mechanical filtration. This type of filter uses as its filter medium a synthetic sponge material. The surface area provided allows the colonization of large numbers of nitrifying bacteria. Various available types of foam and sponge filters all operate on the same basic principle.

The filter is powered by an outside air supply that bubbles in a lift tube, drawing water in through the porous filter cartridge. Water passing through the sponge is filtered and then returned to the aquarium. This filter is primarily suited for small aquariums or quarantine aquariums.

Filter Materials

Biomedia Filter Rings and Blocks

Previously, we discussed filtration and the use of various types of media in filter beds, with special reference made to bioballs, bioblocks, and other media. These specialized types of materials, while not mandatory for filters, are nonetheless useful in various types of filters. The purpose of the media is to make available additional surface area for the bacteria. This effectively increases the biofiltration area, which in turn allows you to accommodate larger numbers of organisms in the aquar-

ium. The design and shape are variable, depending on the manufacturer. Some are in the form of ceramic rings, others plastic blocks, and some are made of ceramic glass foam. For example, the ceramic glass foam type is in the form of a cube and measures $12 \times 20 \times 20$ mm. The equivalent surface area of one of these cubes is approximately 12 square feet (3.65 m^2).

This type of media is also easy to clean during conventional filter maintenance. Generally, all that is needed is to remove the media and rinse under water. It is not recommended that the media be scrubbed, as this could remove the beneficial bacterial biofilm attached to the media.

Activated Carbon

The most commonly available filter medium to remove dissolved organic materials in the water is activated carbon, which is manufactured from various materials including coal and wood. Activated carbon is not the same as charcoal, which has a limited ability to remove organics and should never be used in marine aquariums. Most of the filter media commercially available are high-grade activated carbon.

Activated carbon is extremely porous, with a large surface area and numerous tunnels that trap organic materials. The effectiveness of activated carbon is determined by various factors; in aquariums, two of the most important are the size of the granules and the placement of the carbon in the filter. The smaller the granules, the larger the surface area and therefore the more efficient for removing organics. In addition, the placement of activated carbon is critical. Manufacturers usually indicate that carbon must be placed after the mechanical filtrant (filter floss). This is the correct sequence of filtrant placement. If the activated carbon is placed before the mechanical filtrant, rapid clogging of the carbon can occur, since carbons also act as mechanical filters.

Used in an aquarium filter, activated carbon will maintain crystal clear water and will remove dissolved organics, particulate matter, and compounds that contribute to the undesirable yellow color and odors that can develop in aquarium water. Carbon will also remove common medications used to treat fish diseases. It must be noted that carbon will remove trace elements, but not as much of them as are removed by protein skimmers. With regular water changes, the trace elements removed should be inconsequential and not detrimental to the aquarium inhabitants.

Prior to placement in the filter, all carbons should be washed to remove small particulate matter and dust particles. The amount of carbon depends on the size of the aquarium and the type of activated carbon. Manufacturers provide starting ranges for the amount of carbon to add to aquariums.

Make sure you purchase a carbon specifically made for use in aquatic systems. Some inferior-quality carbons on the market are actually manufactured for use in air purification. These will tend to leach and release phosphate into the aquarium, and therefore should be avoided. Phosphate concentrations in the aquarium are one factor responsible for the increased growth of algae.

Since the efficacy of the carbon will decrease over time, as a general rule it should be replaced every few months. The replacement time varies with the conditions of the aquarium.

Filter Floss

Filter floss is primarily a mechanical filtrant but also becomes a biological filtrant as nitrifying bacteria colonize the filter strands. The filter media are generally synthetic materials such as dacron or polyester. Enough material is simply layered in a box filter, outside, or in canister filter. The mechanical filtrant is also available as presized and layered pads that are simply added to the particular filter used.

Also available are foam pads that perform a similar function to filter floss. Sold in large pieces in various thicknesses, foam pads can be cut to fit almost any type of filter. Precut filter pad replacements are also sold for use in a particular filter.

Mechanical filter media must always precede activated carbon, if carbon is utilized in the filter. As previously indicated, this arrangement prevents the clogging of the carbon, which would rapidly impair its efficacy.

Other Aquarium Accessories

Air Pumps and Diffusers

Besides filtration, some additional source of aeration is recommended to promote additional gaseous exchange and to help in providing a current. Marine animals, particularly invertebrates, benefit from aeration, which in turn assists good water movement.

A high-quality air pump is also required for powering undergravel filters. Various types of air pumps are available; the majority are the vibrator type. These tend to be relatively quiet and maintenance free. It is important that you do not economize on the air pump, especially if you intend to connect it to other pieces of aquarium equipment. Even if the pump supplies more air than needed, the amount can be regulated with valves. These gang valves channel air to various pieces of connected equipment through flexible plastic tubing.

Air diffusers or air stones are useful for providing additional aeration and more water current. As long as ample filtration is provided through good-quality filters, there will be sufficient water movement and aeration. However, you may wish to add an air stone for additional water movement.

Air diffusers are constructed of various materials, including fused glass beads. Pumped air is released through the porous air stones as bubbles, the size of which can be

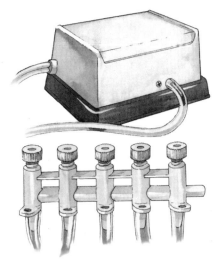

Air pumps (top) are required to power various types of filters and to provide aeration. Gang valves (bottom) are used to distribute the air to air stones and filters.

regulated by the air flow. Depending on the type of stone, a stream of fine or larger bubbles is produced. At the surface the agitation of the water disperses carbon dioxide and other gases and adds oxygen.

Heaters

Marine aquariums should be equipped with thermostatically controlled heaters. A heater ensures that the temperature is maintained within the acceptable range. Some heaters can be secured on the inside of the aquarium by special suction cups; other designs allow the filter to be completely submersible. The temperature is controlled by adjusting a small knob on the heater; a small bulb within the heater indicates when the heater element is functioning.

Heaters are available for all sizes of aquariums, but you must ensure that the heater is correct for use in salt water and that it has ample wattage to heat the aquarium water. Commercial heaters range from 25 watts up to 150 watts.

A rule of thumb for the required wattage is to allow 2 to 5 watts per gallon. The lower range is acceptable if the aquarium is to be kept in a heated room, while the upper range should be used for aquariums located in cool areas. Also consider that the smaller the aquarium, the faster it loses heat. A sample calculation would be for a 20-gallon (75.6-L) aquarium that is situated in a room with normal temperatures throughout the year. Based on this information, $20 \times 2 = 40$ watts. Since heaters are available in standard sizes of 25, 50, 75, 100, and 150 watts, you should purchase a 50-watt heater. If you suspect the room might be much cooler during certain times of the year, you would be advised to use a 75-watt instead of a 50-watt heater.

The recommended water temperature for coral reef fishes is 77 to 85°F (25 to 29.5°C). Higher temperatures should be avoided, as this will reduce the concentration of dissolved oxygen in the water. In some instances, or with some sensitive species of fish and invertebrates from certain regions of the world, such as the Red Sea, the upper range of the temperatures may be required.

Thermometer

An accurate thermometer is a basic requirement. Various types are available; the floating and liquid crystal types are the most popular. Because of possible toxicity, no thermometers constructed of metal or containing mercury should ever be used in marine aquariums. Floating thermometers with liquid mercury could accidentally break and mercury in the water would poison the aquarium animals. The floating thermometers filled with a red alcohol solution are safe to use.

The disadvantage of a floating thermometer is that it freely floats in the aquarium water and you have to find it whenever you want to cheek the temperature. Also, such a thermometer could break if dashed against the side of the aquarium by strong water currents.

A better choice is the liquid-crystal type, available in both Fahrenheit and Centigrade models. These thermometers are thin strips of plastic filled with temperature-sensitive liquid crystals. They are attached to the aquarium glass by a self-adhesive

▶ *Top left: The adult Emperor Angelfish* (Pomacanthus imperator). *Top right: The juvenile Lemonpeel Angelfish* (Centropyge flavissimus) *with a circular marking that disappears as it matures. Center left: The adult Yellow-Faced Angelfish* (Euxiphipops xanthometapon) *should only be kept by an experienced hobbyist. Center right: The Royal Gramma* (Gramma loreto). *Bottom left: The Blackcap Basslet* (Gramma melacara). *Bottom right: The Lyretail Blenny* (Ecsenius midas).

backing. The crystals are activated by heat conducted through the glass from the water, lighting up the appropriate digital readings. Though not as precise as floating thermometers, liquid crystal thermometers are remarkably accurate and do a relatively good job of determining aquarium water temperatures.

Aquarium Cover

All marine aquariums should be covered to limit the entrance of particles and dust, minimize water evaporation, and prevent fish from jumping out. The type of cover required will vary depending on the type of aquarium. Aquarium covers are made of either glass, plastic, or a combination of the two.

An acrylic aquarium requires only the cover supplied with the aquarium to cover the open top area. The light hood can be placed directly on top of such a cover. Other designs incorporate the cover on the bottom of the light fixture.

With glass aquariums, a number of options are available. A full-cover lighting hood covers the entire aquarium and incorporates a lighting fixture. The front portion of such a hood usually has a sliding or hinged glass cover for feeding and performing other required aquarium services.

Another type of cover fits on the ledge inside the aquarium, has a sliding front cover or hinged glass cover, and a rear portion of plastic that attaches to the glass. The plastic can be custom-cut for air-line tubing, heaters, filter tubes, and so on. A separate lighting hood (strip hood) can be placed directly on the cover.

Lighting Requirements

The marine aquarium must receive ample light for several reasons; the most obvious is to allow illumination of the tank for observation of the inhabitants. Also, light is required for the growth of algae, which in turn serve a useful function.

While algae growth was once regarded as undesirable, in marine aquariums it is highly desirable to encourage the growth of some algae. Light is required for normal photosynthesis, growth, and function of algae. Algae should be allowed to grow to yield a supplementary food source for fish, to assist in removal of nitrogen-containing compounds such as nitrate, and to remove carbon dioxide. In addition, certain invertebrates, such as sea anemones and corals, have algal cells within their tissue. Inadequate lighting jeopardizes the survival of these algae, which in turn endangers the survival of the invertebrates.

Various types of reflecting light hoods house the light source—most often fluorescent bulbs. Other types of bulbs, such as actinics, are used especially if the aquarium contains corals and other invertebrates. These bulbs do not give off much heat so they will not heat the water. Other light sources, such as metal halide lamps, cost more to buy and to operate, and many experts consider them unnecessary for adequate light in most aquariums.

For the beginner, the use of a hood equipped with the proper type and number of fluorescent bulbs will supply the necessary light for a marine aquarium. The deeper the water, the more lighting is required for proper illumination and growth of algae.

Marine aquariums should receive 8 to 12 hours of light per day. Those heavily populated with macroalgae may require a longer photoperiod.

The duration, or photoperiod, is only one component of providing proper lighting for marine aquariums. It is also important to understand spectra and intensity as they relate to lighting requirements.

Spectra

Spectra refers to the bands (wavelengths) of light given off by a bulb or other light source. Different bulbs emit different wavelengths of light or colors of light. For example, fluorescent bulbs designed for growing green plants emit more light in the red and blue portions of the spectrum. On the other hand, a daylight-type bulb is deficient in red. Different types of algae, for example, will respond differently to the spectra mix of light emitted by light sources.

Intensity

Intensity refers to the output of light (measured as lumens) from the light source. The number of lumens falling on a square meter area is termed lux. Different types of bulbs with the same wattage can give off different amounts of light. For example, a cool white 40-watt fluorescent tube typically used in aquariums has an output of approximately 4,300 lumens or 107 lumens per watt. On the other hand, a 40-watt plant-type bulb often used to grow plants in freshwater aquariums has an output of 920 lumens or 23 lumens per watt. The cool white gives off more light per watt than the other type of bulb. The number of lumens per watt is termed the lamp efficacy.

Required Bulbs and Illumination

The amount of light required for an aquarium depends on personal preference as well as on the type of aquarium. The appearance of the fish will be different depending on the types of bulbs used for illumination. Bulbs with red in the spectrum bring out the red and orange colors of the fish, while cool white bulbs give fish a more "washed out" appearance due to the deficiency of the red end of the light spectra. For a more desirable appearance of both fish and invertebrates, a few guidelines should be followed when selecting bulbs for illumination.

• There has been a proliferation of types of bulbs for use in the aquarium, as manufacturers continue to improve the quality and output of bulbs. It is important to remember that the lumen output must be within

Tibicen or Keyhole Angelfish.

a certain range for proper illumination and for the growth of macroalgae. Lower light levels encourage the proliferation of undesirable algae such as brown diatoms or blue-green algae.

• A general recommendation is to use two 40-watt daylight fluorescent bulbs, with an output of not less than 60 lumens per watt. This is sufficient to illuminate a 50- to 55-gallon (189- to 208-L) aquarium with fish. If you intend to maintain coral and other invertebrates, additional bulbs will be required for proper illumination. In addition, it is recommended you use a combination of daylight and actinic lamps. Some of the newer fluorescent bulbs combine the features of both daylight bulbs and actinic lighting. A higher lumen output will be required for deeper tanks. Your pet store retailer will be able to recommend the options and required types of bulb you require for your specific aquarium.

Replacing Bulbs

Bulbs used in aquariums have a limited life; over time, their output, as well as the spectrum of the light, will decrease. It is important to note that, although a bulb can still be functioning, its light output could have been greatly diminished. In general, you should replace the bulbs every five to six months. Some manufacturers will be able to tell you that the maximum life of the bulbs is a certain number of hours. If you use a timer for your aquarium lights, you will be able to calculate the expected replacement time for the bulbs based on hourly usage.

Chapter Three

Water and Water Quality

F ish and other marine organisms are directly influenced by the chemical, biological, and physical characteristics of their environment. The water around coral reef habitats is chemically stable because of the large volume of water, the constant currents, wind, and other factors that maintain relative uniformity of the water mass. As a result, reef organisms are not subjected to wide fluctuations in the chemical and physical characteristics of the ocean water. When there is a change it is usually of short enough duration that the animals are not adversely affected.

The situation in an aquarium is radically different. The aquarium water is not subject to constant renewal as in the ocean. In contrast to a coral reef, aquarium water is subject to extensive alterations after the introduction of marine organisms.

The alteration of aquarium water is due to the buildup of chemicals that originate from various biochemical processes, most importantly from the metabolic activities of fish, invertebrates, and algae. If these chemicals are permitted to accumulate to concentrations beyond what the marine animals can tolerate, the survival of the inhabitants will be placed in jeopardy. The toxicity of some of these chemicals is lethal to the inhabitants in very low concentrations, so regular testing of the aquarium water and periodic water changes are crucial for maintaining water quality within acceptable parameters.

Natural Seawater

Seawater is an extremely complex solution composed of numerous chemical compounds, both organic and inorganic. Sodium chloride, or common table salt, is the most abundant inorganic compound in seawater, followed by other major components such as magnesium chloride, magnesium sulfate, and calcium carbonate. Smaller concentrations of trace elements are also dissolved in seawater and include molybdenum, selenium, cesium, vanadium, and zinc. Though these elements are in extremely low concentrations, they are important to the biological processes of many organisms, including algae and invertebrates.

Marine aquariums can be filled with either natural seawater or fresh water plus a synthetic seawater mix. Natural seawater must go through a conditioning process before being used in your aquarium. Natural seawater contains numerous microscopic organisms, both plant (phytoplankton) and animal (zooplankton). If the water is not properly conditioned by dark storage for a few weeks, the death of these organisms could radically alter the chemistry of the water, endangering your aquarium specimens. Secondly, unconditioned water could transmit infectious diseases to your marine fish. Some aquarists prefer to collect their own water, but it is safer and more convenient to use a good-quality synthetic sea salt mix. This is especially true for the new marine aquarist who will find the storage and filtering procedures bothersome and time-consuming.

If you do decide to collect your own seawater, it must be collected away from inshore areas that could be polluted from fertilizer runoff, sewage, heavy metals, insecticides, or other pollutants. Inshore waters also often contain large quantities of suspended particulates. Collect seawater only in nontoxic plastic containers with good-fitting caps. The water should be stored in closed plastic or glass containers for several weeks before use. After storage, you will note on the container bottoms a fine layer of sediment that should not be added to your aquarium. After addition to the aquarium, the water should be subjected to filtration and aeration for several hours before addition of fish. It is also recommended that several water tests be conducted, including pH, ammonia, nitrite, and nitrate to insure that they are within safe levels.

Synthetic Seawater

The invention of a synthetic sea salt mix for keeping marine fish and invertebrates in aquariums was a major achievement that enabled anyone anywhere to set up a marine aquarium. It allowed the convenience of preparing seawater by mixing fresh water with a salt mix. The earlier formulations were inadequate to support fish, and especially invertebrates. Some formulations used inferior grades of chemicals and often some salts did not dissolve completely. Today there are various excellent commercially produced salt mixes that are readily available in aquarium and pet shops. Experience has demonstrated that these synthetic mixes are superior for supporting marine life.

The major advantages of preparing synthetic seawater are that it is free of pollutants and microorganisms that could transmit disease or foul the water, there is no need for storage of extra seawater, and the preparation can be used within a short time after mixing.

To Calculate the Number of Gallons of Water in a Rectangular Aquarium:

a) Measure the aquarium length, width, and height in inches.
b) Multiply length by height by width.
c) Divide by 231.

Example:

How many gallons are in an aquarium with the following dimensions?
47.5 inches (121 cm) long
12.8 inches (32.5 cm) wide
21 inches (53 cm) high

Solution:

$47.5 \times 12.8 \times 21 = 12{,}768$
$12{,}768 \div 231 = 55.27$, rounded off to 55 gallons

Various commercial mixes are available for making seawater. The salt is simply mixed with an appropriate amount of tap water, allowed to mix until thoroughly dissolved, and then the salinity (discussed later in this chapter) adjusted to the acceptable level. Using this method, fish can be introduced to the new aquarium in as little as 24 hours. Although fish can generally be introduced earlier than 24 hours, some salts require longer to completely dissolve.

Water Parameters

Once the fish are introduced to the aquarium water, it will begin to undergo a series of chemical changes, not all of which are conducive to the support of aquatic life. It is therefore crucial to ensure that a high standard of water quality is maintained. Marine animals are extremely sensitive to water deterioration and are not as tolerant as many species of freshwater fish. Without a thorough understanding of the required water quality parameters, you will not succeed as a saltwater aquarist. There are a number of parameters that are critical.

Temperature

Most aquarists will be stocking their aquarium with fish and invertebrates from coral reef habitats. Living coral, other invertebrates, and fish are extremely sensitive to rapid temperature fluctuations. Since fish and invertebrates are cold-blooded, they are directly affected by temperature, which affects their activity, feeding behaviors, immune system, and other metabolic functions. For example, the higher the temperature, the greater the need for food; but this causes an increase of metabolic waste in the water. If there is too low a temperature, activity of the animals slows, there is a reduction in growth rate, and sensitive animals such as corals will die. Such problems, especially the buildup of wastes, does not occur on a coral reef, but in an aquarium they can spell disaster.

Temperature also affects the amount of dissolved gases that directly affect the marine organisms. At a high temperature, less oxygen will dissolve in the water; this affects the respiratory rate of a fish.

The temperature of the aquarium should be constant and maintained within an acceptable range. The range for marine animals is 77 to 82°F (25 to 28°C). This range takes into account the majority of animals that would be maintained in the aquarium. However, for the majority of aquariums stocked only with fish, the recommended range would be

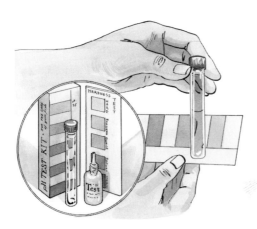

The pH of your tank water can easily be monitored with the help of inexpensive test kits.

77 to 79°F (25 to 26°C). Other aquariums with invertebrates or with marine animals normally found in warmer seas will require slightly higher temperatures.

pH

The pH of water is a measure of acidity or alkalinity. The pH ranges from 0 to 14, with 7 as the neutral point. Above pH 7, water is alkaline; below 7, it is acidic. Because of the complex chemical reactions occurring in the aquarium water, the pH can undergo major shifts.

In nature, the pH of ocean water is usually 8.0 or above, varying with the locality. It is recommended that seawater in the marine aquarium be maintained within the range of 7.8 to 8.3, depending on the type of marine organisms maintained. A pH of 8.0 to 8.3 is a commonly acceptable range for community aquariums with either fish, invertebrates, or both.

Changes in the pH of the water are caused by various chemical reactions and the presence of chemical compounds that slowly accumulate. Several factors in an aquarium contribute to changes in the pH, including the nitrification process, the concentration of carbon dioxide, and the amount of natural buffers.

The nitrification process releases acids that react with bicarbonates to neutralize the acids. Without bicarbonates and carbonates to buffer the water, it would slowly become acid, endangering the aquatic animals. Buffers restrict great change in the pH of a solution. Water in the ocean, which is naturally buffered, has great pH stability. Many synthetic seawaters contain sufficient buffers for the new aquarium. As will be seen later, the type of aquarium bottom material (substrate) is also critical for maintaining the correct pH of an aquarium. Carbon dioxide is also a source of acid in an aquarium, since it forms carbonic acid. Aquariums with inadequate water circulation and aeration can build up excessive concentrations of carbon dioxide.

The general trend of water pH in a stocked aquarium is a continual decrease toward more acidity. Gradual declines are not harmful, but the marine hobbyist must be aware of pH changes to ensure that it does not fall outside of the acceptable range. Various types of bottom materials will help to buffer the water and maintain the pH. However, over time these buffering compounds will become exhausted and will need to be replaced periodically. There are also available special buffering solutions and powders for the aquarium water.

Fortunately, the pH of the water can be monitored by the use of inexpensive test kits. A few drops of an indicator chemical is added to a sample of aquarium water in a test vial. The color of the sample is compared to a color chart that indicates the pH of the water. This test should be run weekly for fully established aquariums, and every few days for new aquariums. A pH kit is essential for all marine aquarists.

Dissolved Oxygen

Aquatic marine animals in nature inhabit an environment with an abundance of dissolved oxygen. In aquariums equipped with proper filtration and aeration, sufficiency of dissolved oxygen is seldom a problem. It is therefore generally unnecessary to test oxygen in aquariums. However, it must be understood that the higher the temperature of the water, the less oxygen dissolves in the water.

Ample concentration of dissolved oxygen is also required for the normal function of the biological filter bed bacteria. The nitrifying filter bacteria are major consumers of dissolved oxygen in an aquarium. In general, it is recommended that the dissolved oxygen concentration be kept near to saturation (maximum amount of oxygen that will dissolve in the water at a given temperature and pressure).

To avoid the possibility of a problem with low dissolved oxygen concentrations, maintain good filtration, avoid overcrowding, and remove any uneaten food from the aquarium bottom.

Specific Gravity and Salinity

The specific gravity (or density) is the ratio of the amount of total dissolved salts in water when compared to pure water. Pure water has a specific gravity of 1.000. As more salts are added to water, the specific gravity increases.

The amount of salt in a marine aquarium is determined by the use of a hydrometer. This instrument is made of a sealed glass tube with an internal scale. The hydrometer is weighted at the bottom and floats freely when placed in water. High-quality scientific hydrometers are standardized against a sea water sample at a known temperature, usually 59°F (17°C). If a reading is taken at any temperature other than 59°F (17°C), the reading must be corrected using a table of correction factors, which are usually provided when you purchase a hydrometer. Such tables also give the salinity value. The temperature must be taken into account, since as water becomes warmer, it expands or becomes less dense.

Other hydrometers are available that are standardized at different temperatures and are more appropriate for use in the tropical marine aquarium. A correction is not required since they have been calibrated at a temperature commonly used for maintaining coral reef fish. Different from the floating hydrometer is one constructed of a narrow plastic chamber with a dial. A water sample is collected in the chamber and the dial indicates the specific gravity. When used according to instructions, a table of corrections is unnecessary. This type of hydrometer is recommended for use in your marine aquarium.

Marine aquarists can determine the correct density (specific gravity) by the use of a hydrometer that has been calibrated for use in the marine aquarium. Two methods are suggested:

1. Reading in the aquarium. Turn off the filters and aeration devices to prevent water movement. Then carefully place the hydrometer in the aquarium and wait until the vertical movement stops. Read the scale at the lowest point where the water level crosses the hydrometer scale. Record the reading and the temperature of the aquarium.

2. Reading outside the aquarium. Fill a tall clear cylinder with a water sample. Carefully place the hydrometer in the water and wait until the vertical movement stops. Read the scale as indicated above; record the reading and the aquarium temperature.

Fish and invertebrates should be maintained in water with a specific gravity of 1.020 to 1.024 at temperatures of 77 to 80°F (25 to 26.6°C).

Specific gravity readings should be conducted every week or two. As water evaporates, the specific gravity will increase, requiring replacement with conditioned tap water. If the specific gravity dips below normal range, you will need to add small amounts of sea salts. This must be done very carefully to avoid too rapid an increase of the specific gravity.

Nitrogen Compounds

Various nitrogen compounds formed in the marine aquarium are generated from biochemical processes including the breakdown of proteins and waste products from marine animals. The principal nitrogen compounds of concern to the marine hobbyists are ammonia, nitrite, and nitrate.

Ammonia

Ammonia is the most toxic product formed in water. It originates from the decomposition of nitrogen-containing organics such as plants and food. Sources of ammonia in the aquarium water are the fish, other organisms, and decaying food.

Ammonia exists in two chemical forms in water: an un-ionized form (NH_3) and an ionized form (NH_4^+). The combination of these two forms is termed total ammonia. Both exist in water, but the proportion of each type is dependent on the pH, temperature, and other factors. The un-ionized form is extremely toxic to marine animals, both fish and invertebrates. The higher the pH of the water, the higher the concentration of toxic un-ionized ammonia.

Chronic sublethal concentrations of ammonia in aquariums indicate that there is a serious problem that can be related to various factors, including overcrowding, filter malfunction, or overfeeding. Fully functional and properly conditioned aquariums should have no detectable concentrations of ammonia.

Ammonia can easily be detected using commercially available test kits. Some kits will express the result as ion, while others will express the result as ammonia-nitrogen. As a general recommendation, the un-ionized form of ammonia must not exceed 0.01 mg/L in marine aquariums. Always follow the manufacturer's instructions exactly to obtain the correct readings for ammonia, regardless of the method for expressing the results.

Nitrite

During the development of nitrifying bacteria in the filter bed, the bacteria will transform ammonia into another form of nitrogen called nitrite. Nitrite is the intermediate step in the nitrogen cycle in the conversion of ammonia to nitrate. The highest concentrations occur during the initial establishment of the filter bed. Once the filter bed is established, it is often impossible to detect any nitrite. Though nitrite is less toxic than ammonia, it is still somewhat toxic to marine animals because it binds with blood cells, which prevents the normal uptake of dissolved oxygen.

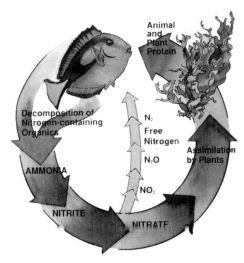

Animal and Plant Protein

Decomposition of Nitrogen-containing Organics

N₂ Free Nitrogen

N₂O

Assimilation by Plants

AMMONIA

NO₂

NITRITE

NITRATE

The nitrogen cycle.

The concentration of nitrite is also determined with a test kit. The concentration should not exceed 0.1 mg/L (parts per million, or ppm) as nitrite ion. Continual high concentrations during the initial conditioning period indicate that the nitrogen cycle is not complete.

Nitrate

Nitrate is formed from the chemical conversion of nitrite in the marine aquarium. It is far less toxic than nitrite and considerably less toxic than ammonia. Although it has been thought that nitrate had little effect on marine organisms, recent research has shown that high concentrations of nitrate can adversely affect the growth and survival of marine animals in the long term.

It is recommended that nitrate not exceed 50 mg/L (ppm), and preferably should not exceed 20 mg/L (ppm) for sensitive invertebrates such as corals. The lower limit is often impossible to achieve in some aquariums. Nitrate levels can be tested with commercially available test kits.

Phosphate

Phosphate, like nitrate, accumulates in aquarium water over time. Phosphates can become a problem if allowed to exceed allowable concentrations. Excessive phosphate concentrations can affect the health of invertebrates as well as contribute to the undesirable growth of algae. The excessive algae growth on rock in reef aquariums will prevent the desirable coralline algae from developing. The concentration of phosphate should be monitored in aquariums. The testing of phosphate in reef aquariums is essential as part of the routine water quality monitoring.

It is important to note that phosphate occurs in both inorganic and organic forms. Many test kits only measure the inorganic form, also known as orthophosphate. Therefore, you can make an erroneous assumption that no phosphate is present if you are using a test kit that measures only orthophosphate. You should check with your pet store concerning the correct type of phosphate kit to purchase.

The source of phosphate originates from three primary sources: utilization of food by the aquarium animals, decay of excessive food, and activated carbon and municipal water. You must be careful about not overfeeding, as this contributes to the buildup of phosphate. Make sure that whenever you purchase carbons they are phosphate-free. Most premium brands on the market will note on the label that the product does not contain phosphate. Tap water should also be tested to ascertain if phosphate is present. If your tap water always contains phosphate, you should consider using deionized water for your aquarium.

Phosphate levels should generally not exceed 0.2 mg/L for aquariums containing fish and 0.1 mg/L if invertebrates are present.

Chapter Four

Setting Up the Aquarium

Once you have purchased the basic equipment, it is time to set up your aquarium. This chapter will give you guidelines for selecting a location and setting up your marine aquarium.

Tank Location

Where the aquarium is placed is a matter of personal preference. It makes a beautiful focus in a living room, den, bedroom, or any other room. Larger aquariums can be placed as an attractive room divider. Wherever you decide to situate the aquarium, it is important to have easy access to multiple wall outlets to minimize the use of extension cords.

The aquarium should not be placed either in an area subject to cold drafts or in one that is excessively warm. Do not place the aquarium too close to a radiator, air conditioner, or directly in front of a window that receives strong sunlight. While several hours of sunlight are beneficial to marine aquariums, strong sunlight can promote excessive algae growth as well as overheating in small aquariums. This is particularly dangerous in the summer months.

The selection of an aquarium stand or cabinet has previously been discussed (see page 7). Regardless of the type of aquarium support, make sure that the aquarium is level to avoid unnecessary stress on parts of the aquarium. This is especially important for all-glass aquariums.

Substrate

The substrate—material to cover the marine aquarium bottom—should be selected carefully. Some bottom materials used in freshwater aquariums are not suitable for a marine aquarium. Freshwater aquariums often use quartz gravel, epoxy-coated rock, or similar materials, many of which are dyed various colors. From an aesthetic point of view, coated or colored bottom substrates should never be used in marine aquariums. Colored substrates detract from the overall natural beauty of the aquarium and

Various substrates are suitable for use in marine aquariums and include a mixture of shells (left), crushed coral (center), and dolomite (right).

reduced surface area compared to smaller-sized particles. This means that there is less area for the beneficial nitrifying bacteria to grow on. On the other hand, very small grains of material such as sand must never be used to cover the aquarium bottom. Sand will rapidly clog undergravel filters and prevent a uniform flow of water through the filter plate. The general recommendation is to select a grain size of 0.12 to 0.2 inches (3 to 5 mm). If no undergravel filter is used, virtually any size of calcareous material can be used to cover the aquarium bottom.

Amount of Required Substrate

The amount of material for an aquarium is mainly dependent on whether you are using an undergravel filter. It is highly recommended that you include an undergravel filter as standard equipment for your first aquarium.

With an undergravel filter a recommended depth of bottom material is 2.5 to 3.0 inches (6.3 to 7.6 cm). This will ensure that you have ample material for proper filtration through your biological filter. You may make the bottom material deeper, but do not make it less than the stated guideline.

In aquariums without an undergravel filter, a shallow layer of substrate is all that should be used to cover the bottom, with a depth of not more than ½ to ¾ of an inch (1.2 to 2 cm) of substrate. The size substrate in this situation is not as critical as with aquariums with undergravel filtration.

especially from the striking coloration of the fish and invertebrates.

Only substrates with a calcareous composition should be used for marine aquariums, since they are the only type that have the capability of buffering the water. The most commonly available appropriate substrates include natural coral sand, limestone, oyster shell, and dolomite. A combination of calcareous materials can also be used for aquascaping the aquarium bottom.

Aquarium bottom materials are essential for proper biological and mechanical filtration when an undergravel filter is used. Large-sized grains of substrate should be avoided, as they inadequately perform mechanical and biological filtration. They also have a substantially

Without an undergravel filter, the bottom material depth must be restricted to minimize the possibility of anaerobic bacterial activity. These bacteria develop in filter beds where there is restricted water flow to carry dissolved oxygen. Without a constant water flow through a filter bed, the substrate favors the growth of anaerobic bacteria, producing toxic gases such as methane and hydrogen sulfide. Both of these gases, even in very low concentrations, are poisonous to marine animals.

Conditioning Water

Unconditioned municipal water is unsafe to use in an aquarium. "Water conditioning" has different meanings, depending on the context. Here the phrase refers to the detoxifying of municipal water that contains toxic chemicals, the most serious being chlorine and chloramine. Tap water can also contain toxic metal ions such as copper, aluminum, or other dissolved materials in concentrations that can be toxic to aquatic life. This can be a particular concern in areas where water districts add copper to water reservoirs during the summer to control algae.

It is essential to treat municipal water with a good-quality water conditioner prior to mixing with sea salts. Water conditioners are available as liquids or powders, with liquids the most popular as they are convenient to dispense. When used

according to instructions, they will destroy chlorine and chloramines within minutes. Some conditioners will also chemically render metallic ions nontoxic if present in the tap water. Some brands of sea salts already contain a water conditioner that destroys chlorine and chloramines while the salts are dissolving. Water conditioners should always be used whenever adding new tap water to the aquarium.

If your aquarium is going to contain some invertebrates, you should consider mixing up the synthetic sea salts using deionized water or RO (reverse osmosis) water rather than municipal water; municipal water supplies can contain other chemicals that can affect invertebrates that tend to be more sensitive than fish. It has already been mentioned that phosphate is one such problem with some municipal water supplies.

Decorating Your Aquarium

The marine aquarium can be decorated or aquascaped in various ways to simulate undersea habitats. You may decide to design a coral reef environment, a reef and lagoon area, or a rocky deep-sea environment. It will be helpful to obtain books or magazine articles with color photos of coral reefs to become familiar with the appearance of the reef environment. With such photos as a guide, you will be

able to construct a more natural and authentic-looking aquarium.

Coral and rock can be arranged to simulate a natural environment and include ample hiding areas, ledges, and crevices for the aquarium fish. Placement of the rock and coral should not be so complex that it will be difficult to remove uneaten food or debris during maintenance.

It is always best to start the arrangement of large pieces of coral rock or other rock at the back of the aquarium. You can build up a wall of rock, then place a few select pieces of coral on some of the ledges. To aid in stabilizing the structure, you can use an underwater epoxy putty for attaching some of the decorations. Commercially available, the putty is easy to use, nontoxic, and cures underwater. It will adhere to glass, rock, wood, ceramics, and metal. The epoxy putty is available in various colors to match with rock or other surfaces.

When you are arranging your decorative materials, work toward the front of the aquarium. Make sure to arrange coral, rock, and other decorations to allow hiding areas, but also to leave ample swimming room for the fish. Be careful to allow enough open areas for a natural water flow to exist, in order to pre-vent buildup of materials at the bases of rocks or coral.

Various types of natural decorations are available to decorate a marine aquarium, including several types of rock such as lava rock, lace rock, and coral rock. There are also decorative items that are replicas of natural coral, sea fans, gorgonia, and sponges.

Living macroalgae make beautiful additions to the marine aquarium; in addition to being decorative, they serve other purposes, including removal of nitrogen compounds. However, depending on the fish and invertebrates, they are not always suitable in all aquariums. Macroalgae are safely added only after the aquarium has been functioning for several months.

Rock

Decorative rock is available in various types, shapes, and sizes. Coral rock is an excellent choice as it will also aid in buffering the water. Lava rock, a light and porous material, is commonly used for decoration. Lace rock, another porous type of rock, is also suitable and commonly available.

It is important to note that not all rock is safe for aquariums. Many contain quantities of soluble metal salts that can quickly kill marine animals. Only rock that you purchase should be used in a marine aquarium. Do not use any rock that you have collected unless you can be certain that it is nontoxic. All rock should be washed well to remove

◀ Top left: The Hardy Goatfish (Parupeneus multifasciatus). *Top right: The Yellow Goby* (Gobidon okinawae) *is a bottom-dwelling fish that lives among coral branches. Bottom left: The Neon Goby* (Elacatinus oceanops) *is a popular Caribbean species. Bottom right: The Porkfish* (Anisotremus virginicus).

any sand or dirt prior to adding to your aquarium.

Natural Coral

The most frequently used decorative item in a marine aquarium is coral. Various types are available, including brain coral, finger coral *(Porites),* staghorn coral, and organ pipe coral.

Any purchased coral should be soaked in fresh water prior to use to ensure that all organic material has been cleaned before being placed in the aquarium. Coral from pet shops is often pretreated and cleaned prior to sale. Such coral can be used after it has been rinsed to remove any dust or other materials that have adhered to the coral skeleton. However, it is still recommended that you subject it to a special cleaning process. This ensures that all organic material has been removed from the coral prior to placement in the aquarium.

First, the coral should be placed in a nonmetallic bucket in a warm area with fresh water to completely cover the coral for at least 72 hours.

If the water is still clear after 72 hours, and no odor is discerned, the coral can safely be removed, rinsed, and added to the aquarium. However, if you notice a film on the water, a cloudy appearance to the water, or a bad odor, remove the coral pieces, rinse well, and process as follows:

• Place the coral in a bucket using 8 ounces (0.2 L) of household bleach for every gallon (3.78 L) of water. Use caution in adding the bleach to avoid getting it on your clothes or in

your eyes. The coral should soak in this solution for 7 to 14 days, depending on the piece of coral.

• After this soaking period, change the water, rinse the coral well, and allow to soak in fresh water for another 24 hours.

• Continue to change the water and allow the coral to soak until you no longer smell any trace of chlorine.

The removal of chlorine from the coral can be hastened by adding a chlorine-removing water conditioner to the water in the bucket. Leave for several hours, then remove the coral, rinse, and place in the sun to dry. When completely dry, smell the coral. If no chlorine odor is detected, the coral can be safely placed in the aquarium. If any chlorine is detected, it will be necessary to soak the coral again in fresh water and treat it again with a water conditioner.

Coral Replicas

Concern for the destruction of coral reefs throughout the world has prompted alternatives to using natural coral in aquariums. Various alternative decorative items are available, including replicas of various species of coral. The replicas are molded from casts made from actual pieces of coral. So lifelike are the replicas that it is difficult to tell the difference between the replica and an equivalent natural piece of coral.

In addition to conservation, these corals have many other notable advantages. They are made of nontoxic materials that will not alter water pH, are lighter in weight than corresponding pieces of natural coral, and are tinted to closely resemble living coral.

Miscellaneous Decorations

Other decorative objects can be used in the marine aquarium; however, please note the following precautions:

• Driftwood found on a beach should not be used; it could pollute the water.

• Shells that have been collected are safe provided they are washed thoroughly before being placed in the aquarium.

• Clam shells and scallop shells are acceptable.

• Snail shells found washed up on a beach can also be used, but care must be taken to ensure that they do not contain remains of the living animal.

• All shells should be washed thoroughly under running water to remove dirt or other material before placement in the aquarium.

Algae in the Marine Aquarium

The growth of encrusting or filamentous algae will impart its own decorative effect within the first few weeks after setting up your aquarium. In the first years of marine aquarium keeping (the early 1950s), the most beautiful marine aquariums were thought to be those devoid of unsightly green algae. Perfectly cleaned aquariums with large amounts of white coral were not uncommon. Today we know that the presence of a certain amount of algae is necessary for the success of a marine aquarium.

The growth of algae in aquariums performs beneficial functions, including the production of oxygen and the removal of various nitrogen compounds like nitrate as well as phosphate. In addition, encrusting algae that cover the rock, coral, and sides of the aquarium provide an excellent supplementary food source for many fish and invertebrates. Many marine animals require algae in their diet for their survival and good health.

Algae are different from other plants in that they lack true roots, leaves, and stems. Algae can be single-celled or multicellular. Algae are classified into three major groups: green, red, and brown. Of the three, the green algae are the most desirable for marine aquariums, but they are more difficult to grow than other types. Green algae require ample light to grow and flourish.

A good growth of green algae in an established aquarium is also an excellent indicator of adequate light and good water quality. However, other types of algae that will grow in the aquarium are brown and red. These are more tolerant of poor water conditions and low light levels.

Once your aquarium has been in operation for a week or more, you will undoubtedly begin to notice a brown color on the substrate, rock, and coral. This process is quite normal and is the first stage in establishing the aquarium. The brown color is primarily due to the growth of microscopic golden-brown algae called diatoms. Since they require very little light to develop and are tolerant of various types of water conditions, they are able to reproduce rapidly. However, if ample light of the correct intensity is provided for at least eight to ten hours daily, you will notice the development of green algae that will replace the growth of diatoms. This will usually begin within several weeks to one month, and will first be noticeable on the rock or coral closest to the light source. With the correct conditions, the green algae will slowly replace the brown algae and red algae, if they also have grown during the first few weeks.

If growth of green algae does not begin within a month, the cause may be inadequate light intensity or duration, water quality problems, or not enough green algae cells to start the growing process. Green algae cells are usually introduced with the fish or invertebrates. If the light and water quality appear to be correct, it may be necessary to obtain a small culture of algae from your retailer. All that is needed is a small amount of green algae removed from a rock or glass and placed in the aquarium.

Keeping Algae Growth in Check

Although some algae are beneficial in aquariums, certain factors can cause an undesirable overgrowth. The accumulation of phosphate, too much light, and a lack of herbivorous fish and invertebrates can result in a problematic growth of algae. As the aquarium becomes established, various species of algae can establish themselves and become troublesome. Filamentous types of green algae can rapidly proliferate and become especially troublesome. The first step to take to control these algae is always to remove as much of them by hand, to prevent too rapid a proliferation. Common species of filamentous algae found in aquariums include *Bryopsis, Cladophora, Derbesia,* and *Enteromorpha.*

Bryopsis is dark green, and is characterized by featherlike tips. It grows in tuftlike clumps on hard surfaces such as rock or on the aquarium glass. It is a persistent alga and difficult to eradicate once established. It is not readily fed on by many herbivorous fishes.

Cladophora is a dark green alga that grows in thick, tangled tufts. Herbivorous fish such as tangs can control these algae as well as snails.

Derbesia, also known as hair algae, are the algae most commonly seen in aquariums. They grow in a mat form, often dense with a variable color. They are much lighter green than other algae and can also appear in a bubblelike form. *Derbesia* is best controlled by herbivorous fish and snails.

Enteromorpha, also a filamentous form, is light green in color and is often one of the first algae to become established in aquariums. It appears as tubular filaments, and easily grows on glass as well as rock surfaces. It often appears and disappears as the aquarium becomes further established. As with many other algae, it is easy to control biologically by means of herbivorous fish such as tangs.

Macroalgae

The familiar encrusting algae are not the only type that will grow in marine aquariums. There are many other types of higher algae called macroalgae (large algae) that make attractive decorative additions.

Several species of macroalgae are commonly available for aquariums. The most suitable types, based on availability and hardiness, are species of *Caulerpa, Penicillus, Udotea,* and *Halimeda.*

As with other algae, macroalgae require ample amounts of light for their proper growth. When first introduced to the aquarium, it is recommended that they receive continuous light for 48 hours. This will help establish them in the new environment.

Like fish and invertebrates, macroalgae do poorly if not provided with good water quality, filtration, and water circulation. For the best growth, the water must have the correct concentrations of nutrients and trace elements. Regular water changes generally are sufficient to satisfy the nutrient needs of macroalgae. However, heavy growths of certain macroalgae such as *Caulerpa* will require the regular addition of trace elements. Various solutions designed for the growth of macroalgae are available commercially.

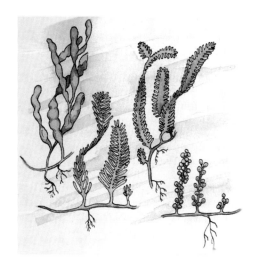

Various types of macroalgae make beautiful additions to the marine aquarium. The attractive Caulerpa spp. *are readily available and grow well in aquariums. Left to right:* C. prolifera, C. ashmeadii, C. mexicana, *and* C. racemosa.

Caulerpa: Various species of *Caulerpa* are the most prolific of the macroalgae and the easiest to grow. This alga grows by the production of rhizomes that develop holdfasts for attaching to the aquarium substrate, coral, or rocks.

Only a growing portion of the plant is required to start *Caulerpa* in the aquarium. Although there are various species available, the following are of particular interest for propagation in an aquarium. Once they are established, they usually grow so rapidly that regular harvesting of the algae may be necessary every few weeks.

These algae are a favorite food of many herbivorous fishes and invertebrates. The plant will be difficult to establish in aquariums with such animals, which constantly nibble at the new shoots. Sea urchins can demolish a good growth of *Caulerpa* within a short time.

Caulerpa prolifera: This species has flat green blades (leaflike portions of the algae) that arise from a horizontal growing stolon, or budding runner. The stolon is attached at irregular intervals to the bottom by small rhizomes. This species has been successfully grown in marine aquariums in Europe for many years. It is the easiest species to grow, even for the beginner. This species is native to Florida and adjacent waters, where it grows abundantly on sandy and muddy bottoms.

Caulerpa ashmeadii: This is a personal favorite, a macroalgae that is very decorative. The blades are feathery, the young shoots light green, darkening as they mature. It is a larger species than *Caulerpa prolifera*. It is also native to Florida and occurs in shallow to deeper water of near 100 feet (30 m).

Caulerpa racemosa: This algae plant is quite different in appearance from other species of *Caulerpa*. Its blades resemble clusters of grapes. It is a common algae found growing on sandy and muddy bottoms in shallow waters off the Florida coast.

Caulerpa mexicana: This species is also featherlike, but has a smaller and more compact appearance. The blades are flattened and are not as broad as in *Caulerpa ashmeadii*.

Penicillus, Udotea, and Halimeda: These genera represent some of the calcareous algae, each with varying degrees of calcification. The calcium in their tissues gives them a degree of rigidity and sonic protection from being eaten by herbivorous fishes. They are much slower growing than *Caulerpa*. These genera are also good indicators of an important water quality parameter: calcium. If sufficient calcium is present, they will flourish.

Penicillus capitatus: This is commonly referred to as the Shaving Brush. The thick stalk of the alga is crowned with a large tuft of thin filaments. The tufts of young plants are light green, whereas in mature plants the filaments become calcified and can take on a white appearance. This species of algae is found growing on sandy or muddy bottoms in Florida and adjacent waters.

Udotea spinulosa: This small species is known as the Mermaid's Fan and is an attractive addition to the aquarium. Unlike various species of *Caulerpa,* it is not a favorite food of many plant-eating fishes. It is one of several species sold for marine aquariums. The stalk of this alga is thin, with a broad fan-shaped blade. It is native to the Bahamas and Florida waters.

Udotea flabellum: This species resembles *Udotea spinulosa* but has a thicker stalk. It is native to Florida waters.

Halimeda opuntia: This tropical alga is sometimes called the Money Plant or Sea Cactus. It is composed of highly calcified connecting segments resembling a type of cactus.

▲ *Left: The adult Domino Damselfish*
(Dascyllus trimasculatus). *Right: The*
Sebae Clownfish (Amphiprion sebae)

It occurs in Florida and adjacent
waters and is found growing on
sandy areas and coral reefs.

Procedure for
Setting Up the
Aquarium

At this point your aquarium
should be situated in a selected
location and on its stand, aquarium
cabinet, or some other support.
Before proceeding, check again that
the aquarium is level and properly
located. Once you fill the aquarium,
you will not be able to move it.
Never attempt to reposition an
aquarium with water; this can cause
the aquarium to crack or burst.

A small-sized aquarium can be
set up in several hours if everything
is prepared and ready to be assem-
bled. A new aquarium should be
rinsed well with plain tap water to
remove any dust or particulate matter. No soap, detergents, or any
other cleaning chemical should be
used; such household products,
even in low concentrations, are toxic
to marine animals. When this is
complete, the aquarium is ready to
be checked for leaks. This is best
accomplished by filling with tap
water and waiting for 24 hours. If
leaks are detected, the aquarium
should be returned for replacement.
Otherwise, completely drain the
water and proceed with the following suggested steps. Due to the various types of equipment available for
aquariums, you will need to modify
the following set-up procedure for
your own situation. The following
does assume you are using an
undergravel filter. If you are using a
hanging type of trickle filter, a protein skimmer, or other equipment,
you should install this last on the

After adding the substrate, add water carefully to avoid disturbing the substrate.

be equipped with a one-way check valve. This will prevent accidental siphoning of the water from the aquarium in the event of a power failure.

2. The substrate must now be washed prior to placement in the aquarium. Bottom materials generally have large quantities of dust and other materials that will cloud your aquarium water. The bottom material should be washed in portions, under running water, in a clean plastic bucket. Do not use a bucket that has previously been used to hold any type of soap or household chemicals. It is recommended that you purchase a nontoxic plastic bucket solely for use with your aquarium. While the water is running, mix the substrate continuously, then pour off the turbid water. Repeat the procedure until the water runs clear.

3. As the bottom material is washed, begin adding it to the aquarium over the undergravel filter. Be very careful not to get any of the bottom material underneath the filter plate. Depending on how you are going to decorate the aquarium, you can either make a level layer of substrate or slope it upward toward the rear of the aquarium.

4. Add enough water to fill the aquarium to about one third of its depth with tap water. Be very careful not to disturb the filter bed or get gravel underneath the filter plate. Begin by arranging the larger pieces of rock or coral in the aquarium. Delicate pieces of coral need not be added at this time. Add tap water to

aquarium. Aquarium setups that already have a predrilled aquarium bottom with a trickle filter in the stand require only a minimum of steps for installation.

If you are using an undergravel filter, install the filter plate first; otherwise, wash the substrate as outlined in the next part of this procedure. If you are not using an undergravel filter, the substrate depth should be less than 1 inch (2.54 cm) in depth under most situations.

1. Once the filter is positioned, insert the supplied airlift tubes according to the manufacturer's instructions. Then position the air pump and cut a sufficient length of tubing to reach a gang valve for distributing and regulating the air flow to the various outlets. Cut the proper lengths of air tubing for connection to the undergravel filter. It is important to note that the air pumps must fill the aquarium at least halfway with water.

5. Once this is accomplished, add the amount of synthetic sea salt required for your aquarium. Many brands of sea salt need not be dissolved before adding to the aquarium.

6. You can now fill the aquarium to within several inches from the top. The water will be cloudy at this point; however, you need not be concerned, as it will clear once the salt has been completely dissolved. Also add the recommended amount of a commercial water conditioner to destroy any residual chlorine or chloramines.

7. Finish connecting the air tubing to the undergravel filter and air pump. After the connections are made, plug in the air pump. Adjust the gang valve so as to deliver enough air to produce a steady stream of bubbles. As a safety precaution, make sure your hands are completely dry before plugging in any electrical equipment to avoid the danger of shock. Salt water is an efficient conductor of electricity.

8. If an outside trickle filter or other filter is used, attach it to the outside of the aquarium, add washed activated carbon, filter floss, or other materials, then plug in the filter. If a canister filter is being used, prepare the filter with the appropriate filter media.

9. Position the heater on the back or side of the aquarium and plug into

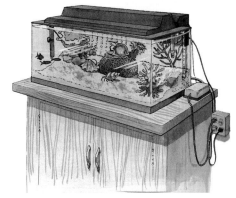

Be sure to run your aquarium filter a few days before introducing new fish.

the electrical socket. Make the necessary adjustments according to the manufacturer's instructions.

10. Complete your aquarium by adding the rest of the equipment, such as an air diffuser, protein skimmer, and fluorescent light hood.

It is highly recommended that filters operate for a minimum of 24 hours to permit proper dissolving of the sea salts and to allow the water to clear. After 24 hours, you should check the specific gravity of the water. Adjust the specific gravity as required by adding either additional salt or additional tap water. The temperature of the heater should also be adjusted to ensure that the temperature of the water is within the acceptable range.

After a final check to verify that all equipment is in operation, you are ready to introduce your first aquarium fish.

Chapter Five

Selecting Marine Fish

Once your aquarium has been properly set up and the filter and other equipment are in operation, you are ready to acquire some marine animals. This section will present the procedure for selecting fish and a brief survey of various families of fishes and representative species.

Numerous species of fish are available from specialty tropical fish stores; however, not all fish sold are easy to care for under aquarium conditions. Some species, for example, are particularly sensitive to water conditions and do not adapt easily to a new aquarium. These fish are best added after the aquarium has been functioning for several months. Other fish have specialized feeding requirements, such as a supply of live foods, and thus require more care to maintain them in the best of health.

It is suggested that you become familiar with the various families, their characteristics and behavior, environmental needs, and food

◄ *A Candy-striped Shrimp* (Lysmata ambionensis) *cleaning a Meyer's Butterflyfish* (Chaetodon meyeri).

requirements. It is important in the beginning to restrict your selection to hardy species of fish and initially to purchase only a few specimens. Once you have gained enough experience in keeping these fish alive, you can then slowly add additional fish to your collection.

Carrying Capacity of Aquariums

The carrying capacity simply means the total number of animals that can be safely maintained in your aquarium. Determining exactly how many fish and invertebrates can be maintained in an aquarium is not simple. To determine this scientifically requires data on weight of the marine animals, the type of substrate, water temperature, various water quality parameters, and other factors. This is impractical and bothersome, especially for a new aquarist.

There are rules of thumb for how many inches of fish per gallon of water can be safely kept in a tank. A general recommendation is 2 inches (5 cm) of animal for every 10 gallons (37.8 L) of properly filtered water. This takes into account the correct number of filters, good aeration, and other factors. For the new aquarium, the rule of thumb is fairly safe to follow to minimize the buildup of toxic nitrogen such as ammonia in new aquariums.

For a new 20-gallon (75.6-L) aquarium equipped with an undergravel filter and outside filter, I would suggest no more than two or three fish about 2 to 3 inches (5 to 7.5 cm) in size. Once the aquarium has been set up for several months and is properly functioning, you can add additional animals, including a few invertebrates.

Purchasing Fish for the Aquarium

The new marine hobbyist should exercise caution in selecting stock for the aquarium. Retail pet stores, many of which specialize in tropical fish, stock large numbers of marine animals. The selection of healthy specimens requires good observation and an ability to ask pertinent questions about the health and behavior of each fish.

Selecting Fish

1. Take your time in looking at the wide variety of species available and choose several specimens. Once you have narrowed your choice to a few fish, make careful mental notes about the fish's behavior. Is the fish swimming normally? Is it active? If the fish is sluggish or has difficulty swimming, it could be a sign of an impending problem. Then pay particular attention to the eyes, skin, and fins. The eyes of a healthy fish should be clear, not cloudy. The skin should be normal and free of discolored areas or reddened lesions. The fins should be clear and intact, with an absence of frayed areas. The latter problem may have been caused by a fight with another fish in the tank, or it could signify a bacterial infection.

2. Note the overall physical appearance of the fish, especially the abdominal area. Healthy fish that have been feeding well have normal, rounded, full bellies. If the head appears enlarged or the abdominal area thin, chances are that the fish has not been feeding well. Avoid the purchase of any specimen with questionable physical appearance.

3. You should also note any sign that suggests the fish is already diseased. For example, never purchase fish that have small white spots on the body or fins. This could be coral reef disease or saltwater ich, caused by a small parasite. As we will discuss in a later chapter (page 135), this disease and others can rapidly kill new fish.

4. When you have selected the fish, ask your retailer a few additional questions that will help make the transfer of the fish to the new aquarium easier on you—and the fish. Have the retailer verify that the species of fish you have selected are

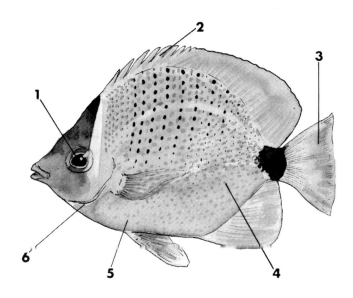

Signs of good health:
1. clear appearance of eyes
2. absence of frayed areas
3. intact fins
4. normal coloration (no discolored or reddened areas)
5. firm and rounded appearance
6. normal, steady respiratory rate

compatible with each other in the aquarium.

5. Ask how long the fish have been at the store and what type of food the fish have been eating. It is a good idea to purchase some of the same type of food for initial feeding of the fish in your aquarium.

6. You should also obtain water quality information from the retailer, including temperature, salinity, and pH of the water in which the marine fish have been maintained.

Introducing New Fish into Your Aquarium

The marine fish you have purchased will be carefully packed with a small amount of water in plastic bags with an overlay of air. Packed properly, your fish will be safe for several hours or more. Certain stores may pack the fish with an overlay of pure oxygen, which allows the fish to remain in the bag for much longer periods without danger of oxygen depletion.

It is important that the fish not be chilled during the trip from the store to your home aquarium. Upon arrival, place the bags in a warm area and make a last-minute check that your aquarium is functioning properly. Check the temperature to ensure it is within the acceptable range. If your aquarium lights are on, it is recommended that these be turned off during the time you will be transferring the fish into the aquarium to reduce stress and shock to the fish.

Place the bags with the fish in the aquarium to begin the transfer procedure. The purpose of floating the bags in the aquarium is twofold: to equalize the temperature of the water in the bag and the aquarium, and to adjust the pH of the bag water closer to the pH of your aquarium water.

The entire procedure should not take more than 35 to 45 minutes, depending on the initial conditions. If the temperature and pH of the bag water and your aquarium water are similar, the procedure can be accomplished in as little as 15 to 20 minutes.

Once the bags are floating in the aquarium, open them to allow air exchange. After the first 10 minutes, add some aquarium water into each bag. Then every 10 to 15 minutes add a little more aquarium water. After 35 to 45 minutes, you will be ready to introduce your new fish into the aquarium.

It is best to avoid adding the water in the transport bag to the aquarium. To introduce the fish into the aquarium, use a soft, fine net. Dispose of the water and the bag. Never reuse bags in which fish have been transported.

It is best to keep the aquarium light off until the next day. After introduction into the aquarium, the fish will undoubtedly seek a sheltered area behind a rock or a piece of coral, a quite normal fright response. Give them some time, and they will be out and about.

The Acclimation Period—The First Few Weeks

The first few weeks after the addition of new marine fish are the most critical period. During this period they will either adapt to their new environment or perish. Also during this period they are most vulnerable to stress and water quality problems. You must use extreme care to be sure that the animals are maintained within the recommended water parameters (pH, temperature, specific gravity, and so on). (See Procedure for Setting Up the Aquarium, page 43.)

Keep in mind that your new fish will be frightened by the transfer and their new surroundings. It will take time for them to adapt to the new environment. You must ensure, especially for the shy fish, that there are adequate hiding areas and refuge from aggressive behavior. It is quite normal for your fish not to eat for several days, so you should not become overly concerned. As the fish adapt, they will venture forth from behind pieces of coral, and then start to eat.

Community Aquariums

The selection of fishes is critical for a harmonious community aquarium. Some species are perfectly compatible with members of their own species, some will not tolerate others of their kind, and still others are altogether unsuitable for community aquariums and must be kept by themselves.

One of the most important problems with marine fish is the pronounced aggressiveness and territoriality of some species. It is a major reason why they should not be crowded in an aquarium.

For all of these reasons it is important to become acquainted with the behavior of various types of fish and to not overcrowd them.

Territoriality

Territoriality, which is a form of aggression, is common among coral reef fish in nature. This behavior tends to become intensified when these fish are in closer confinement in an aquarium. Inappropriate selection of fishes for an aquarium can result in a chronic problem and the eventual death of some of the fish.

Territorial behavior is expressed by coral reef fish by the establishment and defense of specific areas that in nature can vary from a few feet to several yards or more. Behavioral reactions evoked by an intruder to a defined territory include chasing, nipping, and dramatic color changes. In general, the behavior of the fish guarding a site involves patrolling the area, with regular visiting of boundaries. The degree of this patrolling behavior varies with the species of fish and other factors.

The territorial behavior of coral reef fishes can be subdivided into two types: aggression toward different species of fish, and aggression toward the same or related species. The first type would be, for example, aggression between a clownfish (*Amphiprion* sp.) and a damselfish (*Dascyllus* sp.). The second type of aggression would be exemplified if several specimens of the Threespot Damselfish (*Dascyllus trimaculatus*) were placed in an aquarium. Within a short time, there would be aggression within the group as each attempted to define its own territory. Such behavior is related to the need for space by coral reef fishes.

Dominance Hierarchies

Another behavior phenomenon in an aquarium is dominance hierarchies. In this system, a number of fish of the same species in an area establish a pecking order. A larger fish will chase a smaller fish, that fish will chase the next smaller, and so forth. This is common among various species of fish, especially damselfish.

Maintaining Fish Compatibility

Maintaining the compatibility of numerous species of fish in an aquarium can be a problem. While incompatibility cannot always be eliminated, it can be minimized by following some general recommendations.

A basic requirement is to become familiar with the general behavior of various families of fish. Secondly, avoid crowding of aquarium fish. Aquariums should be decorated to provide ample shelter areas with the use of coral rock, coral, lace rock, and the like. The placement of these items must provide boundaries between different areas of the aquarium.

When choosing species of fish it is also recommended to include varied sizes, coloration, body shapes, and habitat requirements. Select a mix of fishes, with some that normally swim in open water and some that prefer to inhabit the bottom areas of the aquarium. This approach usually minimizes aggressive tendencies.

It is also advisable to avoid the introduction of only one or two fish to an aquarium in which a group of fish have been living for some time; it is better to introduce a number of new fish at once. This is due to the fact that in an established aquarium, territorial areas have already been defined by the resident fish. Introducing a single new specimen causes the other fish to view it as an intruder. Such a fish can be chased and nipped violently enough to cause injury. To minimize risk, it is best to add a new fish during a time when the aquarium is being cleaned, the coral is removed for washing, or the decorative items are rearranged. The disruption with the rearrangement of the aquarium decor sometimes allows a new specimen to go unnoticed. Presumably, the other fish are so busy redefining their own

territories that the new specimen does not become a focus for aggression.

A Survey of Aquarium Fish

Numerous coral reef fishes available for marine aquariums are collected all over the world—from both coasts of Mexico, the Philippines, the Red Sea, the Indian Ocean, Fiji, Indonesia, and Sri Lanka. Aquarium fishes are also collected in Florida and Hawaii. With such a diversity of species, you may find it hard to confine your choice. Some fish are commonly available for home aquariums, while others are not often seen for sale. The fish in short supply command a much higher price.

Closely related species of fish are grouped into families. Members of such families share common physical characteristics and behavior. With so many families of fish and thousands of species, it is impractical to discuss all of them in this book. This section, therefore, discusses some of the most common families of fishes and many of the species generally available in tropical fish stores.

A suitable approach to choosing aquarium fish is to become familiar with each of the families of fish in this section. Review the various species and then decide which fish interest you most. As you will see, more care is needed for certain fish, such as those that require live food exclusively. Many species, however, are relatively easy to care for and will eat a variety of food.

In your initial selection, avoid the temptation of buying a fish known to be more difficult to care for. Wait until you have proved that you can properly care for the hardier fish before attempting to care for more difficult species.

Angelfishes
(Pomacanthidae)

The angelfishes include numerous beautiful and colorful species. They are distributed throughout the world's tropical seas; most, however, are found in the Indo-Pacific, the Red Sea, and adjacent areas. They are most common around coral reefs, patch reefs, and rocky areas.

Angelfishes are one of the most popular aquarium fishes. Although some appear to be delicate, the majority of angelfishes are quite hardy and have excellent longevity records in aquariums. They do require ample room in an aquarium, as many species are territorial. To avoid territorial disputes and fighting, only one specimen of a species should be kept in an aquarium.

The coloration of angelfish varies greatly among species and even between juveniles and adults of the same species. For example, the juvenile French Angelfish *(Pomacanthus paru)*, a popular aquarium species, is laterally compressed with a black body and vertical yellow stripes. By contrast, as the adult matures, it loses the yellow stripes and the body scales become outlined in yellow.

The majority of angelfishes are good eaters, consuming a wide variety of animal and plant materials. They adapt well to aquarium conditions. You should not purchase very young fishes; they are susceptible to diseases and if kept with larger and more aggressive fish, may starve. Juvenile angelfish may be fussy eaters.

The Koran Angelfish *(Pomacanthus semicirculatus)* is a readily available and excellent aquarium species. The coloration of juvenile specimens varies, depending on the age of the fish. They are primarily dark in color with a series of semicircular white bands and blue markings. This angelfish is a good eater, accepting a wide variety of foods.

The Emperor Angelfish *(Pomacanthus imperator)* is one of the most sought after of all angelfishes; however, it is not as hardy as the Koran Angelfish and cannot be considered a fish for the beginner. The adult of the species is sometimes available and must be maintained only in larger aquariums.

Some of the angelfish discussed grow to be quite large and are unsuitable for small aquariums. The pygmy angelfish group, *Centropyge* spp., however, are especially well suited for smaller aquariums. These colorful fish remain small and are very hardy.

The Coral Beauty *(Centropyge bispinosus)* is without a doubt one of the hardiest and most readily available of all the pygmy angelfishes. It is purple with orange on a portion of the body, as well as reddish markings. It adapts well and readily eats various types of foods but must be provided with algae, which it consumes in the natural habitat.

The Flame Angelfish *(Centropyge loriculus)* is another hardy pygmy angelfish. It is a brilliant red, with dark ventral markings on the body. It is well suited for the beginner. This species must also be supplied with algae to graze upon in the aquarium.

The Lemonpeel Angelfish *(Centropyge flavissimus)* is more difficult to maintain and is recommended only for aquariums with an abundant growth of green algae. Algae are a major component of this species' diet in the natural habitat. The fish is a beautiful yellow, with light blue around the eyes and along the gill plate.

Basslets (Grammidae and Pseudochromidae)

The basslets are small, colorful fishes, always in great demand as aquarium fish. They are found in the tropical Atlantic and Pacific. In nature they inhabit coral reefs and rocky areas. Basslets are predatory, feeding on invertebrates, planktonic crustaceans, and occasionally on small fishes. The basslets are a hardy group that usually prospers in marine aquariums.

Fairy Basslets (Grammidae) from the Atlantic are limited to five species, with the readily available Royal Gramma the best known. The rarer Blackcap Basslet *(Gramma melacara)* is far less often seen for sale.

The Royal Gramma *(Gramma loreto)* is one of the most beautiful and hardy fishes for the new aquarium hobbyist. In nature, it lives on shallow and deep reefs, searching for food in and around caves and under ledges. The color of the Royal Gramma is a brilliant magenta on the forward part of the body and bright yellow on the posterior portion. A dark spot is present on the dorsal fin. Since in cramped quarters it is aggressive toward its own kind, only one Royal Gramma should be kept, unless the aquarium is large enough. With adequate hiding areas it is possible to maintain more than one specimen.

Basslets (Pseudochromidae) from the Pacific, also known as dottybacks, have been popular aquarium fish for many years. In Europe they have been referred to as the pygmy basslets. Over 50 species of dottybacks from the Indo-Pacific and Red Sea are currently known. Like their Atlantic relatives, these fish are small, colorful, and predatory. Their small size, generally not exceeding 7 inches (18 cm), makes them an excellent addition to small aquariums. Like the Royal Gramma, they are territorial, so more than one of the same species should not be kept in small aquariums. The basslets' color, related to the diet, tends to fade in captivity.

Several popular and commonly available species are the Skunk Basslet, the Bicolor Basslet, and the Purple Basslet (or Strawberry Fish).

The Skunk Basslet *(Pseudo-chromis diadema)* is a small brilliantly colored fish with the upper portion of the body violet and the lower portion a bright yellow. It is commonly imported from the Philippines and other areas of the Pacific. In nature, this fish feeds on small invertebrates, including shrimp and worms. Because of their aggressive behavior, only one Skunk Basslet should be kept in an aquarium.

The Bicolor Basslet *(Pseudochro-mis paccagnellae)* is also yellow and violet, but with this species the anterior is violet and the remainder of the body yellow. It is a very aggressive fish and should not be maintained with timid fish such as gobies.

The Purple Basslet *(Pseudochro-mis porphyreus)* is a uniformly beautiful purple color. This fish is the least aggressive of those discussed in this section. In nature, it lives in rubble areas, feeding on small crustaceans and other invertebrates. Like the other basslets, only one of its kind should be maintained in an aquarium.

Batfishes (Ephippidae)

The batfishes are deep-bodied, laterally compressed, slow-swimming fish inhabiting the Indo-Pacific regions. In their natural habitat, they are found in mangrove and lagoon areas, where the young can be mistaken for floating leaves. Their long fins and coloration afford them very effective camouflage.

Batfish should be kept only in large aquariums, as they grow rapidly with a good diet and other favorable aquarium conditions. They should not be with aggressive fishes, especially as juveniles. Batfishes are excellent eaters and will eat foods fed to other marine fish.

The coloration patterns of juveniles and adults differ according to the species. For example, the juvenile Pinnatus Batfish *(Platax pinnatus)* is dark in color with an orange-red line along the anterior edge of the dorsal fin and head to the mouth. The outlined edges are also visible on the other fins. As the fish matures, the coloration changes to a grayish-brown and the markings disappear. The shape of the fish also changes to the more characteristic batfish body shape. The Pinnatus Batfish is a popular aquarium fish. It adapts easily to aquariums, and becomes tame enough to accept hand-feeding. In nature, this fish is known to grow longer than 12 inches (31 cm).

The Long-Finned Batfish *(Platax teira)* is a well-known batfish available for aquariums. It is characterized by exceptionally long fins that gradually shorten as the fish matures. It is brown in color with vertical bands of gray or silver. In its natural habitat, the fish schools in mangrove areas, where it feeds on small invertebrates and algae. As with all batfish, this one should not be kept with aggressive fish, which tend to attack and shred the batfish's fins.

Blennies (Blenniidae)

Blennies are small scaleless fishes that occur as numerous species found in all tropical seas. Most are bottom-dwelling fishes with elongated bodies and modified pectoral fins used to prop themselves on the bottom. Many species also have small projections called cirri on their heads.

These small fishes have not enjoyed the popularity of other fish. They are generally not as brilliantly colored as other popular aquarium fish, but what they lack in color, they make up with their interesting "personalities" and behavior. In the author's opinion no aquarium is complete without one of these active and interesting fish.

In their natural habitat, blennies are found in shallow waters near coastal areas, patch reefs, and tidepools. They tend to be secretive and will dart to safety if disturbed. Blennies have variable feeding habits; some species are carnivorous and others are herbivorous. Carnivorous blennies feed on small invertebrates such as small worms, shrimp, and amphipods. Herbivorous species feed primarily on various types of marine algae.

The majority of blennies adapt well to aquarium conditions and have good survival records in captivity. Herbivorous species must be provided with abundant supplies of algae. All blennies should be supplied with ample hiding places and not combined with overly aggressive fishes. Many blennies are themselves very aggressive and will defend their territories in the aquarium.

Of the more than 250 known blenny species, two of the more popular ones are the Bicolor Blenny and the Golden Blenny. Several from the tropical western Atlantic are also available.

The Bicolor Blenny (Ecsenius bicolor) is solitary in habit and feeds primarily on algae. It lives in coral recesses, but spends time swimming in midwater. It is a beautiful fish, the anterior portion of the body purplish to gray and the posterior portion yellow. The male coloration is more pronounced; the females are darker over the entire body.

The Golden or Lyretail Blenny (Ecsenius midas) is another popular aquarium fish. Like the Bicolor Blenny, this species swims actively in midwater. In its natural habitat, it eats algae and small invertebrates. When maintained in an aquarium, it must be provided with algae to feed on. The color of the fish is an overall yellow with the head region darker, tending to yellow-brown. The fish gets its name from its elegant lyre-shaped tail.

The Redlip Blenny (Ophioblennius atlanticus), an excellent species from the tropical western Atlantic, is a bottom-dweller. It is less colorful than many Pacific species, with overall brown to gray coloration and areas of red, orange, or pink on the body. This species is active in an aquarium, where it feeds primarily on algae. It is very hardy and will adapt very well to most aquarium conditions.

Butterflyfishes (Chaetodontidae)

The butterflyfishes include some of the most popular and beautiful of all species maintained in aquariums. Their beautiful colors, shapes, and graceful swimming behavior are some of the reasons for their popularity. They are widely distributed throughout tropical seas, with the greatest diversity of species occurring in the Indo-Pacific. While many are suitable for the aquarium, a greater majority are more difficult to maintain successfully. Some species are quite aggressive and can inflict damage on their tankmates. Many have specialized feeding behaviors. For example, some species feed only on specific types of coral polyps. For this reason, you should be careful to purchase only species that are known to thrive in captivity. Overall, butterflyfishes do not have the best longevity records in aquariums, with the exception of several species.

Butterflyfishes should be provided ample room in an aquarium, as many species exhibit extreme territorial behavior and aggressiveness toward those of their own kind. As a general rule, butterflyfishes are shy and should not be combined with aggressive tankmates.

Many species are highly sensitive to the nitrite concentrations generally encountered during the initial establishment of the biological filter bed. These fish are therefore not recommended until the aquarium water has been completely conditioned.

Butterflyfishes feed on a variety of foods, but some tend to be highly selective. A varied diet is recommended, including frozen, live, and prepared foods.

Since butterflyfishes are so popular and widely available, a number of the most suitable species will be discussed.

Species of *Heniochus* are among the few butterflyfishes that school in the natural habitat. They adapt well to new aquariums, are readily available, and will accept a diet that includes live, frozen, and dry foods. Although several species are commonly available, some do better in the aquarium than others. In general, all *Heniochus* species thrive better when they are maintained in larger aquariums.

The Bannerfish *(Heniochus acuminatus)* is the best-known species of the six in the genus. In the natural habitat, it usually swims in pairs or small schools. Its diet includes algae, plankton, and small invertebrates. The coloration of this fish is white with broad, vertical black bands; the dorsal fin and tail are a light yellow. The most obvious characteristic of this fish is the long dorsal filament. As the fish matures, it also develops bony bumps on its head.

The longnosed butterflyfishes include the Forcipiger *(Forcipiger flavissimus),* Longnosed Butterflyfish *(Forcipiger longirostris),* and the Copperband *(Chelmon rostratus).* The Forcipiger is laterally compressed like other butterflyfishes, with a long snout. The color of the fish is yellow with a dark coloration on the head and lighter underneath. This fish is omnivorous, eating a wide variety including brine shrimp, pieces of

clam, shrimp, and other foods. It should not be confused with *Forcipiger longirostris,* similar in coloration and appearance but with a slightly longer snout. This species is more difficult to maintain and is not recommended for the new aquarist.

The Copperband Butterflyfish has requirements similar to those of the Forcipiger. It is a light-colored fish with three vertical copper-brown bands. In the natural habitat, it feeds on small invertebrates. It is more difficult to maintain in the aquarium, as it prefers live foods. It is therefore not recommended for the beginner.

The Raccoon Butterflyfish *(Chaetodon lunula)* has a beautiful color pattern and its adaptability to aquariums makes it a good choice for the new hobbyist. Color patterns differ in the juvenile and adult fish. The adult coloration is yellow with a broad black band passing through the eye. Just behind this is a white band from which a black band extends upward. A black spot is at the base of the caudal fin. In the natural habitat, the Raccoon Butterflyfish is found in pairs or small groups. It feeds on coral polyps, small invertebrates, and algae. In the aquarium it readily accepts a variety of foods, including dry flake foods.

◄ *Top left: The Blue-Spotted Jawfish* (Opistognathus rosenblati). *Top right: The Moorish Idol* (Zanclus canescens). *Center left: The Bicolored Parrotfish* (Cetoscarus bicolor). *Center right: The Striped Burrfish* (Chilomycterus schoepfi). *Bottom Left: The Stars-and-Stripes Puffer* (Arothron hispidus). *Bottom right: The Foxface* (Siganus unimaculatus).

The Threadfin Butterflyfish *(Chaetodon auriga)* is also a popular species well suited for the home aquarium. The fish is white and yellow with a broad black band through the eye. The adults of the species have a trailing filament on the dorsal fin; the filament is absent in young fish. It feeds on a wide variety of foods on the coral reef, including algae, shrimp, worms, and coral polyps. It has a habit of biting and tearing bits from bottom-dwelling invertebrates for food.

Numerous other species of butterflyfish are sold for home aquariums, but many are poorly adapted to the home aquarium. Many species are so strict in their feeding requirements that it is difficult to provide them with the foods they need on a regular basis. For example, sonic species feed exclusively on coral polyps. They will eat other foods offered but generally do poorly and begin to decline in health within several months. Since it is often impossible to keep a continuous source of coral to serve as food, these fish are not recommended for aquariums. Those that should not be purchased include the Ornate Butterflyfish *(Chaetodon ornatissimus)* and the Meyer's Butterflyfish *(Chaetodon meyeri).*

Cardinalfishes (Apogonidae)

The cardinalfishes, widely distributed throughout tropical seas, are small, predatory fishes, and are characterized by their large eyes, elongated or compressed bodies, and large mouths.

Cardinalfishes vary in color from red to brown, many with distinct color patterns. They are nocturnal in the natural habitat, feeding on small invertebrates and fishes. During daylight, cardinalfish retreat under ledges or crevices in the coral.

Several species of cardinalfish will do well in home aquariums. Their predatory feeding behavior inclines them to live foods, but they will accept frozen shrimp, clams, and fish. Their nocturnal behavior also requires ample hiding areas or small caves.

The Pijama Cardinalfish *(Sphaeramia nematoptera)* is a readily obtainable popular fish from the Pacific Ocean. In the natural habitat this species is found in small groups hovering over the reef where it feeds on small invertebrates. It is brown, with red eyes and a diffuse to dark band through the body. The posterior portion of the body has a series of reddish-brown spots. This cardinalfish does well in an aquarium and several can be maintained with no problem of aggression among themselves. A small group of them in a large aquarium is particularly striking.

The Gold-Striped Cardinalfish *(Apogon cyanosoma)* is another popular fish from the Pacific. It is also nocturnal and feeds on small invertebrates and fishes. The Gold-Striped Cardinalfish has a series of longitudinal yellow-gold stripes on a background body color of brown. It is also a good choice as an aquarium fish.

The Banggai Cardinalfish *(Pterapogon kauderni)* is a popular and striking-looking fish, with its black and white coloration and extended fins. Native to the islands off Sulawesi, Indonesia, this fish has become a favorite of aquarium hobbyists. It is a hardy fish and readily breeds in captivity. It will accept frozen and dried foods.

Several species of cardinalfish are collected in the tropical Atlantic. They include the Flamefish *(Apogon maculatus)* and the Barred Flamefish *(Apogon binotatus)*. The Flamefish is bright red with a series of dark markings on the body. In the natural habitat this fish is commonly found near rock ledges and among the spines of sea urchins. The Flamefish is a popular aquarium fish. The Barred Flamefish is similar in appearance to the Flamefish, but has a lighter body color and two dark bands on the posterior portion of the fish.

Damselfishes (Pomacentridae)

The damselfishes are classified into numerous genera and species and include the popular Domino Damselfish, Blue Chromis, and the anemonefishes. As a group the damselfishes are among the easiest fishes to maintain in a marine aquarium. They are long-lived, not very particular about the types of food offered them, active, colorful, and generally inexpensive. These characteristics make them a perfect choice for the new marine aquarium. They are commonly purchased as the first fish for an aquarium because of their hardiness and ability to survive the conditioning period.

However, there are a few disadvantages you must keep in mind. The majority of these fishes are highly territorial and aggressive toward their own kind as well as other, unrelated species. Even their small size does not prevent them from defending a territorial area from fishes much larger than they.

Anemonefishes: The highly colored anemonefishes or clownfishes are unique in that they associate with sea anemones in the wild. The relationship affords an advantage principally to the fish, which receives protection from predators. The anemonefish secretes mucus with a chemical substance that deters the sea anemone from discharging its stinging cells. Sea anemone venom is toxic to other fish upon contact with the tentacles. Anemonefishes do not require a sea anemone in the aquarium to do well, but the coexistence adds beauty and interest to the aquatic community.

Various species of anemonefishes are regularly available from tropical fish stores. The following species are recommended for the home aquarium.

The Ocellated Clownfish *(Amphiprion ocellaris)*, a relatively nonaggressive and colorful fish, is a readily obtainable species. The fish has an orange body with broad white bands. This species is one of numerous marine fish that are bred commercially for the aquarium trade. It is one of the easiest clownfish to maintain in a home aquarium and is highly recommended for the new hobbyist.

Although it is not a requirement, it is intriguing to keep a sea anemone with this species. This clownfish accepts a wide range of foods and is compatible with other fishes.

The Maroon Clownfish *(Premnas biaculeatus)*, another popular species, has a maroon body and a characteristic spine just below its eye on the gill cover. This species is known to be very aggressive in aquariums, and not more than one should be kept in a tank, since it will fight with other members of its species. However, the Maroon Clown fish does well in an aquarium and has an excellent longevity record.

The Sebae Clownfish *(Amphiprion sebae)* is a popular and easy fish to maintain in the marine aquarium. The fish's dominant color is dark brown with three broad vertical bands across the body. The pectoral fins are yellow; the remaining fins are black. The coloration changes as the fish matures.

Other Damselfish: The other genera and species in this family are colorful, active fishes with aggressive, territorial tendencies. In the native habitat, the various species tend to remain close to coral outcroppings, rocky areas, and areas of refuge. Some species school, however, and swim over the reef proper. The majority of the popular species for aquariums belong to the genera *Dascyllus, Pomacentrus, Chromis,* and *Chrysiptera.*

The Domino Damselfish *(Dascyllus trimaculatus)* is readily available and one of the most commonly imported species. It is black in color with three white spots; as the fish matures, the spots begin to fade. This species feeds well in aquariums and has an excellent longevity record. Domino Damselfish will become more aggressive as they mature and should therefore not be kept with timid or shy fishes.

The Three-Striped Damselfish *(Dascyllus aruanus)* is an attractive aquarium fish, with alternating white and black bands and a transparent tail. It is a very hardy fish, perfect for the beginner's aquarium. In the natural habitat, individuals are found around coral branches. This fish is omnivorous, feeding on a variety of animals and plants.

The Blue Damsel *(Pomacentrus coelestis)* is a popular, bright blue fish. This Indo-Pacific species is hardy, feeds well, and is one of the best beginner fishes. It is not as aggressive as the pugnacious Three-Striped Damselfish.

The Green Chromis *(Chromis caerulea)* is a peaceful, schooling damselfish. The dominant body color is light blue-green. In the natural habitat, these fish swim over the reef in schools, where they feed on planktonic organisms. In aquariums, they are best kept in schools as well. Green Chromis should never be kept with aggressive fishes.

The Atlantic Blue Chromis *(Chromis cyanea)* is a Caribbean schooling fish with a blue body and forked tail. This fish lives in open water over the reef, feeding on planktonic organisms. Like the Green Chromis, this fish should not be kept with aggressive fish that are apt to nip its fins and disrupt normal feeding.

Dragonets (Callionymidae)

The dragonets are small bottom-dwelling fish inhabiting coral reefs and adjacent areas. They are a unique group of fishes, with the Mandarin Fish *(Synchiropus splendidus)* being the best known of the dragonets. Another species, the Spotted Mandarin *(Synchiropus picturatus),* is also available in the aquarium trade. Both species are collected in the Pacific, with large numbers collected in the Philippines.

Mandarin Fish in their natural habitat feed on small invertebrates such as worms, amphipods, and shrimp. They frequent coral reefs and adjacent sandy bottoms in pairs or small groups.

Their coloration is extraordinary. The Mandarin Fish shows various shades of orange and green, with greenish bands edged in black. There are blue markings on the fins. No description can do justice to the gaudiness of these complex color patterns.

Neither species can be considered easy to maintain, and neither is recommended to the inexperienced aquarist. These fish tend to fare better when kept in the minireef type of aquarium, where they can hunt among the coral and rock and feed on small invertebrates. Their tiny mouths mandate very small pieces of food. They relish live foods such as brine shrimp and tubifex worms. Frozen brine shrimp are also excellent. Since these fish are slow feeders, they will not do well in an aquarium with aggressive fish. When provided with proper conditions, however, these fish are quite hardy.

Drums and Croakers (Sciaenidae)

The drums and croakers are aptly named; they are able to produce sounds using muscles near their air bladder. These fishes are distributed throughout tropical and temperate seas. The drums found in the Caribbean are the only fish in this family (Sciaenidae) that are popular as aquarium fish. Drums are slow feeders, with the juvenile specimens tending to be timid. Drums will not be able to feed well if combined with aggressive fish and will slowly starve to death.

The High Hat *(Equetus acuminatus),* also known as the Cubbyu, is occasionally available for sale. The body is black and white with a black dorsal fin. Young specimens have a long and pronounced dorsal fin that shortens as the fish matures. In the natural habitat, High Hats are found near patch reefs, and the juvenile specimens can be found among the protective spines of the sea urchin (*Diadema* sp.).

In aquariums, the High Hat will do well as long as it is not combined with aggressive fish. More than one fish of the same kind can be maintained together with no problems of aggression. It is intolerant of poor water quality and should not be introduced into the aquarium until it has gone through the complete conditioning cycle. Rocky areas and small caves should be provided as refuge. High Hats will eat a variety of foods, including worms, clams, and shrimp.

The Jackknife Fish *(Equetus lanceolatus)* is another drum that occurs in the tropical western Atlantic. The fish is light gray with distinctive dark bands on the body. It is not as commonly available as the High Hat. In an aquarium it has requirements similar to other drums, but is more difficult to keep. It is not recommended for small aquariums or for the beginner.

Goatfishes (Mullidae)

Goatfishes are active bottom-feeding carnivorous fishes. In their natural habitat, they are found in sandy or rubble reef areas, where they feed on small invertebrates. The fishes are characterized by a pair of sensory barbels that help to locate their prey.

Goatfishes are not as colorful or as popular as other aquarium fish; however, they are not territorial. They are hardy and always active in the aquarium, feeding on pieces of food on the bottom. Various species from the Indo-Pacific and the tropical Atlantic are commonly sold for stocking aquariums.

The poor longevity record of goatfishes has been attributed to starvation. If these active fishes receive their share of an adequate diet, they do very well in community aquariums.

The Goatfish *(Parupeneus multifasciatus)* is a popular species from the Philippines. It is pink with areas of yellow, and three broad bands of black on the body. Another species, the Band-Tailed Goatfish *(Upeneus vittatus)* is also commonly available. This fish is found in small groups near coral reefs, feeding on small bottom-dwelling crustaceans, including crabs and shrimp. The fish is gray to silver with four to five longitudinal yellow stripes. A series of dark bands are on the dorsal fin.

Several interesting goatfishes are also available from the tropical Atlantic and include the Yellow Goatfish *(Mulloides martinicus)* and the Spotted Goatfish *(Pseudupeneus maculatus).* Both species are suitable for aquariums when obtained as juvenile specimens. They have requirements similar to other goatfishes.

Gobies (Gobidae)

The gobies are a large family of fish found in tropical, subtropical, and temperate seas. Many species, but not all, have modified pectoral fins that form a suckerlike attachment organ. In the natural habitat, gobies can be found in rocky areas and sandy bottoms. Some species are solitary and some can be found in small groups.

Gobies are relatively easy to maintain, and though some species are delicate in appearance, they are hardy and do well in aquariums. As a rule, gobies are shy and should not be kept with overly aggressive fishes.

The Fire Goby *(Nemateleotris magnifica)* is a popular and commonly available Pacific and Indian Ocean species. It is beautiful, with a pearl-colored body, fiery red markings on the tail, and a tall dorsal spine. It is shy and in the aquarium requires refuge areas. The Fire Goby should never be combined with aggressive fish, which have a habit of biting off the high part of the dorsal fin.

A closely related species is the Purple Fire Goby *(Nemateleotris decora)* from the western Pacific. It is pale gray to pink, with areas of bright blue and red on the fins. The dorsal fin is elongated, but not as long as the Fire Goby's. Like the Fire Goby, this species does well in the aquarium when maintained properly and fed a variety of foods including brine shrimp and shrimp.

Some of the smaller bottom-dwelling gobies are in the genus *Gobiodon.* The Yellow Goby *(Gobiodon okinawae)* inhabits coral branches in the natural habit. Its pelvic fins are modified for adhering to rocks, ledges, and coral. These gobies are excellent aquarium fish and feed on a variety of foods.

The Neon Goby *(Elacatinus oceanops)* is a popular and well-known Caribbean species inhabiting reef areas, patch reefs, and lagoons. The Neon Goby is dark with a bright blue horizontal band on each side. These fish are often found in pairs. This goby is one of the few species of fish to have been bred successfully in captivity.

Neon Gobies are "cleaner fishes," those that are known to clean parasites clinging to other fish. In nature, Neon Gobies can be observed swimming around moray eels, groupers, and other fish, where they pick off attached parasites. Large fish such as groupers will allow the "cleaners" to roam freely over their bodies, even allowing them to enter their mouths to remove parasites.

Grunts (Haemulidae)

The grunts are classified into various species found in tropical seas. Like the drums, they are capable of producing sound. They accomplish this by grinding their pharyngeal teeth. These patches of teeth occur on the upper and lower portions of the gill arches. The sound is amplified through their swim bladder, producing a gruntlike noise.

In the natural habitat, grunts can be found in shallow waters and on the reef. Many species school and are often found in large numbers on the reef during the day. At night, they scatter to adjacent sandy areas to feed. Primarily predators, grunts feed on bottom-dwelling invertebrates, including worms, clams, and shrimp.

Not all kinds of grunts are suitable for aquariums. However, the young of several species will adapt fairly well to a community tank.

The Clown Sweetlips (Plectorhinchus chaetodonoides) is a popular aquarium fish from the Pacific. Though the adult grows large and is not particularly attractive, the juvenile is beautiful. Young fish are brown to orange, with large white areas edged in black. They have large dorsal and tail fins and swim in a graceful pattern. As the fish matures, the coloration changes drastically to a gray. The Clown Sweetlips is an excellent eater and does well in the aquarium. It should not be kept with shy or timid fish.

Of the tropical Atlantic species, the Porkfish (Anisotremus virginicus) is beautiful, with a yellow body, two black bands on the head, and blue stripes on the posterior. It is nonaggressive, so several can be kept with complete compatibility among themselves and other tankmates.

Most other species of grunts are not recommended for aquariums and require large tanks to do well. As a rule, with the exception of the two species discussed, grunts cannot be considered suitable for the smaller marine aquarium.

Hawkfishes (Cirrhitidae)

The hawkfishes are a small group of predators found primarily in the Indo-Pacific. They are aptly named, as they perch on coral branches or rock, waiting to pounce on their prey. In the natural habitat, hawkfish feed on small crustaceans, fish, and other invertebrates. They are generally solitary.

Hawkfishes are small with elongated bodies, small mouths equipped with teeth, thickened pectoral rays, and strikingly beautiful coloration. They often have small hairs, or cirri, on the tips of the dorsal spines.

The Freckled Hawkfish (Paracirrhites forsteri) is a beautiful and hardy fish. It is variable in color with an overall dusky to white body with a longitudinal reddish-brown band. Small dark spots are distributed on the head. In the natural habitat, this predator feeds on small fishes and invertebrates. The Freckled Hawkfish is a popular aquarium fish. Because of its predatory behavior, it must not be kept with fishes smaller than itself.

Another popular hawkfish is the Fire Hawkfish, sometimes referred to as the Flame Hawkfish *(Neocirrhitus armatus).* It is imported from the Indo-Pacific and the Red Sea. It is red with a black band along the base of the dorsal fin and around the eyes.

One of the most interesting hawkfish eagerly sought by marine aquarists is the Longnosed Hawkfish *(Oxycirrhites typus),* which uses its long snout to probe small crevices for food. In the natural habitat, this hawkfish lives in deeper waters, generally greater than 100 feet (30.3 m). It is found perched on gorgonians and soft corals, and in rocky areas. It feeds on a variety of small invertebrates, including crustaceans and worms. The fish is white with a crosshatched pattern of shades of red.

Hawkfishes adapt well in aquariums, are quite hardy, and are not difficult to feed. They are especially suited to smaller aquariums. It is recommended that they be introduced into the aquarium after the completion of the conditioning cycle, since they are highly sensitive to ammonia and nitrite.

Jawfishes (Opistognathidae)

Jawfish are carnivorous bottom-dwelling fishes that live in burrows in shallow water. They have elongated bodies, with large eyes, large mouths, and small scales. Various species are known from the Atlantic and Indo-Pacific. Many jawfish live in colonies, although each inhabits its own burrow. The size of jawfish ranges from 5 inches (13 cm) to the over 1-foot (30-cm) length of the Giant Jawfish *(Opistognathus rhomaleus)* from the eastern Pacific.

Two species are particularly popular as aquarium fishes, the Yellowhead Jawfish *(Opistognathus aurifrons)* from the Caribbean Sea and the Blue-Spotted Jawfish *(Opistognathus rosenblati)* from Mexico.

The Yellowhead Jawfish is a beautiful species common to the tropical western Atlantic. This fish is small, with a maximum size generally not exceeding 4 inches (10 cm). The fish is bluish-white, with blue fins and a yellow head. In the natural habitat, it feeds on small crustaceans. The fish is hardy and does well in aquariums.

The Blue-Spotted Jawfish reportedly lives in large colonies of over 100 fish. It inhabits rocky or rubble-strewn bottoms in shallow water. The fish is orange-yellow overall with electric-blue spots distributed over its body. The male is known to develop a different coloration during breeding, when the rear part of the body darkens. This species also does well in aquariums and has requirements similar to other jawfishes.

Jawfish must be supplied with a sufficient depth of bottom material in which to construct their burrows. A minimum of 4 to 6 inches (10 to 15 cm) of bottom material should be supplied. Jawfish are always busy collecting pieces of gravel, pebbles, and shell to maintain their burrows.

Since jawfish fare poorly in aquariums with aggressive fish, tankmates must be carefully chosen. These fish have a legitimate reputation for jumping out of the aquarium, so the top of the tank must be completely covered. Jawfish should be fed brine shrimp, plankton, pieces of fish, clams, and the like. Live foods, including adult brine shrimp, are a favorite.

Moorish Idols (Zanclidae)

This genus has only one species, the Moorish Idol (Zanclus canescens). These fish are common in small groups on Pacific and Indian Ocean coral reefs. In the natural habitat, they feed on small invertebrates and algae. Their small brush-like teeth and the snout are used for browsing in crevices and small holes.

The Moorish Idol has a pointed snout and a characteristic high dorsal fin with a trailing filament. It is white with two broad bands of black on the body. The tail fin is black with blue edging; there is an orange mark on the snout.

This fish is highly sought after for aquariums, despite its poor longevity in captivity. Though beautiful, the Moorish Idol is definitely not for the beginning marine hobbyist; even advanced hobbyists have difficulty maintaining this fish. It requires a diversity of foods, including small crustaceans and some algae. The temptation to purchase this fish should be resisted until you have become sufficiently experienced with keeping other species.

Parrotfishes (Scaridae)

Parrotfishes are herbivores with a strong parrotlike beak formed from the fusion of their teeth. They are found in all tropical seas. In the natural habitat, parrotfish can be observed biting or scraping algae from encrusted coral or biting off pieces of coral. The algae are digested and the pulverized coral is excreted as fine sediment.

In the natural habitat, these fish are solitary or in groups. Some species are known to school. Many parrotfish also have an unusual habit of secreting a cocoon of mucus at night during their inactive "sleep" period.

The coloration of parrotfish depends on the sex. The females tend to be less colorful than the brightly colored blue or green males.

Adult parrotfish can measure more than 2 feet (61 cm). Although some species are sold regularly as juvenile fish, as a rule, they are not recommended for aquariums, with the exception of a few species. However, even these should be maintained in larger tanks.

The Bicolored Parrotfish (Cetoscarus bicolor) is a favorite among marine aquarists. In the natural habitat, this fish lives in shallow waters, feeding on algae. The adult coloration is green; the body coloration of the juvenile is white with a brown posterior edge, an orange head, and a black spot on the dorsal fin.

The Blue-Spotted Parrotfish *(Leptoscarus vaigiensis)* is also imported as small juvenile specimens. To do well in captivity, like other parrotfish, this fish needs adequate algae in the diet. The fish is brownish, with blue spots distributed over the body.

Parrotfish should not be kept in aquariums with living coral, which can be consumed when the fish scrape for algae. For the most part, parrotfish should be maintained only by experienced aquarists and in larger aquariums.

Porcupinefishes (Diodontidae)

A highly unusual family of fishes, these spine-laden creatures have the ability of inflate themselves and erect their spines if disturbed or

When frightened, the porcupinefish can inflate itself and erect its spines to ward off enemies.

frightened. They have large eyes and powerful teeth. In the natural habitat, porcupinefishes feed on crustaceans, including small shrimp, crabs, lobsters, and other invertebrates. These fish are found in shallow waters near patch reefs and in lagoons.

Several species are suitable for marine aquariums. The Porcupinefish *(Diodon hystrix)* is a commonly available species for aquariums. The fish is gray-white with dark spots distributed over the body. It is an excellent and hardy aquarium fish when obtained as a juvenile.

The Striped Burrfish *(Chilomycterus schoepfi)* is a popular Caribbean species. It has a whitish body with brown stripes and a few large brown spots, and green-blue eyes. The spines of this species are erect at all times. This particular species is easy to feed and becomes quite tame, readily accepting food from your fingers. It will get along with other fish in community but may become aggressive with fish smaller than itself or with members of its own kind. It is a very hardy fish that will do well under various conditions.

Their powerful jaws and chisel-like teeth easily crush small hermit crabs, crabs, shrimp, and other invertebrates. They should never be kept in aquariums with small invertebrates, which they will seek out and consume.

These fish are excellent eaters and should be fed a variety of foods, including pieces of frozen or fresh shrimp, crab, fish, clam, and mussel.

Pufferfishes (Tetraodontidae)

The puffers are a large, diverse group of omnivorous fishes widely distributed in tropical and temperate seas. In the tropics, they inhabit coral reefs, adjacent areas, and lagoons. These slow-swimming fishes are characterized in part by their elongated and stout bodies, rough skin, small fins, and modified teeth. They lack body spines. Their strong teeth are used for crushing crabs, shrimp, mollusks, and other invertebrates for food. They have an ability to inflate themselves with water or air if disturbed or frightened.

Several species are suitable for aquariums when obtained as small specimens. Pufferfishes are not recommended for the new marine aquarist, especially if the aquarium is to be a fish and invertebrates community aquarium.

The Reticulated Puffer *(Arothron reticularis)* from the Indo-Pacific inhabits shallow reefs and sandy areas. It feeds on small invertebrates. It is not a particularly colorful fish, having a body with a reticulated pattern of brown stripes on a white body. It is available from time to time in tropical fish stores.

The Stars-and-Stripes Puffer *(Arothron hispidus)* is so called because it has spots (the "stars") and, on the lower body, stripes. It is a carnivorous fish with an appetite for feeding on coral, crabs, worms, and other invertebrates. It is certainly not a good choice for reef-type aquariums with many invertebrates. How-ever, it is an interesting fish that adapts well but should be kept in an aquarium with fish only. The fish is primarily brown or gray, with a distribution of white spots over the anterior portion of the body. A series of narrow white stripes are usually present on the ventral part.

Puffers are not difficult to maintain in the aquarium, but they are very aggressive with members of their own species. They may also tend to bully and take bites out of the fins of other fishes. Pufferfishes should never be kept in aquariums with invertebrates, which they will quickly devour.

These fish are easy to feed with a wide variety of foods, including clams, shrimp, dry foods, and pieces of fish.

Rabbitfishes (Siganidae)

The rabbitfishes are a small family, occasionally available to marine aquarists. Rabbitfishes are primarily herbivores. They are typically found browsing on algae, in small groups or in pairs on coral reefs, patch reefs, and areas of high vegetation. These fishes are widely distributed in the tropical Pacific and Indian Oceans.

The rabbitfishes are characterized by a laterally compressed ovoid body, small scales, and a prominent head and mouth.

Several species are recommended for aquariums, the best known being the One-Spot Foxface *(Siganus unimaculatus)*. The fish's body is predominantly yellow-brown or bright chrome yellow, with the head region white. A broad band of black passes through the eye on an angle with black on the breast area. A conspicuous black spot is sometimes present on the side below the dorsal fin.

Another rabbitfish is the Barhead Rabbitfish *(Siganus virgatus).* In the natural habitat, the fish typically school as juveniles. The fish is brownish-yellow, with a series of blue lines on the head. Two bands of black pass through the eyes and at the base of the pectoral fin.

Rabbitfish adapt well to aquariums and are quite hardy. They tend to be aggressive toward members of their own species; otherwise, rabbitfish are excellent for the beginner's community aquarium, as they tolerate a wide variety of water conditions. Since they are herbivorous, they must be provided with ample algae upon which to browse. They will also accept most other types of foods, including plankton and dry flake foods.

Be warned that rabbitfish are equipped with venomous spines that can inject a small amount of venom if the handler's skin is punctured. Avoid contact with spines of the dorsal, anal, and pelvic fins.

Scorpionfishes (Scorpaenidae)

The scorpionfishes are a large group consisting of the lionfishes and stonefishes. The stonefishes are the most venomous fishes known. The scorpionfish, like the rabbitfish, are capable of delivering poison through hollow spines. The wound is painful but usually not life-threatening. Stonefish, however, are capable of delivering enough poison to produce a very painful lesion. If one is allergic or in frail health, the risk is greater.

Only the lionfish will be discussed here, as they are the only fishes in the group that are of major interest for the home aquarium.

Lionfish, once referred to as turkeyfish, are among the most beautiful fishes known. They possess long flowing fins with an array of colorful markings. They have been popular with hobbyists for many years. In the natural habitat, lionfish can be found on reefs and adjacent areas, hiding under ledges and in crevices. All scorpionfishes prey on small invertebrates and fish.

Various species in several genera are sold as aquarium specimens. The Volitans Lionfish *(Pterois volitans)* is magnificent, with red body coloration and alternating white and brown-red vertical bands. Since this fish will quickly devour fishes smaller than itself, tankmates must be selected carefully. It should be maintained in larger aquariums, as it grows very quickly when provided good environmental conditions and the proper diet.

The Zebra Lionfish *(Dendrochirus zebra)* is one of several smaller species; it reaches no more than

▶ *Top: The small Harlequin Sea Bass* (Serranus tigrinis) *is hardy and long-lived in an aquarium. Bottom: The beautiful Threadfin Snapper* (Symphorichthys spilusus) *is native to the Philippines.*

8 inches (20 cm) and it is more suitable for smaller aquariums. The fish has a pinkish body with a series of red-brown stripes. Like the other lionfish, it requires live food.

The Fu-Manchu Lionfish (Dendrochirus biocellatus) is another favorite. It has a white body with reddish bands and two large dark circular areas (ocelli) edged in yellow. Like other scorpionfish, it is hardy and usually adapts well.

In general, any of these fish makes a beautiful, hardy, and long-lived addition to the home aquarium. Since their dorsal spines are hollow and can inject venom, care must be taken in moving these fish or working in the tank.

These fish will generally eat only live food. If the fish are obtained while juveniles, they can usually be trained to take pieces of shrimp or fish. It is recommended that lionfish be kept only by experienced aquarists.

Sea Basses (Serranidae)

This large family of carnivorous fishes are distributed worldwide, primarily in warm seas. The sea basses include a variety of genera and species, from large groupers to the small, highly colored anthiid fishes. In the natural habitat, they feed on fish and crustaceans. The sea basses are quite hardy, but many species require large aquariums due to their large size and rapid growth. Since they are predatory, they must not be kept with fishes much smaller than themselves.

One of the most popular and attractive species is the Pantherfish (Cromileptes altivelis). The body is gray-white with numerous dark spots. In the natural habitat, the Pantherfish is found in pairs or solitary. Small juvenile specimens are excellent for the home aquarium and do well with other fish; however, their rapid growth requires a large aquarium. The Pantherfish is aggressive and will readily devour any fish smaller than itself; therefore, a choice of tankmates must be made carefully.

The Miniatus Grouper (Cephalopholis miniata), from the western Pacific and Indian Oceans, is also imported for aquariums. It is fiery red with small blue spots distributed over its body. Like the Pantherfish, it should be only in larger aquariums. It is hardy and does well in an aquarium when acclimated, but it grows rapidly because of an almost endless appetite.

The smaller Harlequin Bass (Serranus tigrinis), native to the Caribbean, is one of the easiest sea basses to maintain in an aquarium. Though not very colorful, it makes a hardy and long-lived aquarium fish.

The Anthiinae, a subfamily of the Serranidae, are still smaller sea basses. Brightly colored, they are eagerly sought after as aquarium fish. The males tend to be a different color from the females. These fish are found in the tropical Pacific and Indian Oceans. In the natural habitat, these fishes are found in large aggregations around coral reefs, where they feed primarily on plankton.

There are various species of sea basses available commercially for the marine aquarium. A well-known, commonly available species is the Square Anthias *(Pseudanthias pleurotaenia)*. The males are reddish-pink and the females an overall yellow-orange color.

A more commonly available species from the Philippines is the Purple Queen *(Pseudanthias tuka)*. It is breathtaking in its coloration. The female is purple, with a narrow band of yellow extending from the back to the tail fin. The lower portion of the fish is also outlined in yellow. The male is purple with a darker purple on the dorsal fin.

The Anthiids are not as easy to maintain as many other coral reef fishes. They are best kept in small groups rather than solitary. They are not recommended for the new marine aquarist. Anthiids are sensitive to water conditions and should not be added until the aquarium is completely conditioned. They prefer live foods but can be trained to accept other types, including frozen and dry foods.

Sea Horses and Pipefishes (Syngnathidae)

This family is comprised of some of the best-known fishes. These are widely distributed in tropical and temperate seas. The majority of the species are sold from the Indo-Pacific and the Caribbean. Although these fish are popular, they are more difficult to maintain due to their requirements for live food. Many species do not do well unless they can have a continuous supply of live

food. They are not recommended for the new hobbyist.

Sea Horses

Sea horses are unusual in that they swim erect, primarily using their dorsal fin and pectoral fins for propulsion. Their prehensile tail permits the fish to remain secure while resting and feeding. In the wild, sea horses feed continuously on small shrimp, amphipods, isopods, and copepods; therefore, they must be fed frequently in the aquarium in order to survive.

Since sea horses are slow feeders, they do poorly in community aquariums with fast-feeding fishes. Sea horses are not territorial, allowing large numbers to be maintained successfully in an aquarium. The key to success in keeping sea horses is nutrition. Most beginners attempt to feed them primarily brine shrimp, which is known to be of poor nutritional value. This can be rectified by simply enriching the brine shrimp prior to feeding your sea horses (see Nutrition section, page 119). This step will ensure that your sea horses are receiving the proper nutrients to grow and thrive in the aquarium.

Sea horses vary in color and often change in color, with some brilliant yellow, orange, or bright red. Sea horses, like pipefishes, are peculiar in that the male is equipped with a brood pouch in which the females deposit their eggs for development. After the eggs hatch, the male gives birth to the young.

Several species of sea horses are regularly available for aquariums.

The Dwarf Sea Horse (*Hippocampus zosterae*), from Florida, Cuba, Bermuda, and the Bahamas, is small and does well especially in aquariums strictly devoted to maintaining them, perhaps with a few other small fishes and invertebrates. The adults seldom measure more than 1½ inches (3.8 cm). This species requires a diet of live food such as *Artemia* (brine shrimp). It has a short life span, reportedly no more than a year.

Larger sea horses, such as the Longsnout Sea Horse (*Hippocampus reidi*) and the Atlantic Sea Horse (*Hippocampus erectus*), are particularly suitable for marine aquariums. These fish grow to 6 inches (15 cm) or more. In the natural habitat, they can often be found in turtle-grass beds. Like the Dwarf Sea Horse, they require live foods, including adult brine shrimp, small fish, or small grass shrimp. Pieces of coral and the like should be supplied so they can attach for feeding.

Pipefishes

Pipefishes and the closely related sea horses share a number of similarities; however, while sea horses swim upright, the slender pipefishes swim horizontally. Although some are colorful, the majority range from gray to olive-green.

Of the species available, the most popular is the Harlequin Pipefish (*Doryrhamphus dactyliophorus*), commonly imported from the Pacific and Indian Oceans. This pipefish has alternating white and red-brown bands on the body and a small red

tail. It is an active fish, especially in reef-type aquariums, where it hunts around coral for small shrimp and other crustaceans.

As with other fish in this family, they must receive live food such as brine shrimp. They should not be kept with aggressive fish.

Snappers (Lutjanidae)

The snappers are a large family of predatory fishes found around coral reefs in tropical seas. Some species can attain a size in excess of 3 feet (1 m). In the natural habitat, snappers feed primarily on small fish and a variety of invertebrates including small shrimp. Snappers are usually night predators.

Most snappers are unsuitable for the typical home aquarium, although some species adapt well as juveniles.

One of the most popular and beautiful snappers is the Emperor Snapper (*Lutjanus sebae*). The juvenile has vertical maroon and white bands on the body. As the fish matures, the bands are lost and the fish's color becomes more uniform and pale.

The Emperor Snapper is hardy and a good choice but should be maintained only in a large aquarium. It may soon outgrow a small aquarium. In the natural habitat, it is known to grow to more than 3 feet (1 m). It is a voracious eater of small invertebrates and fishes smaller than itself.

The Blue-Lined Snapper (*Lutjanus spilurus*), another Pacific species, is also suitable when obtained as a juvenile. The fish has a yellow body with five longitudinal blue stripes.

This fish has requirements similar to other snappers.

A most striking snapper is the Threadfin Snapper *(Symphorichthys spilurus),* imported from the Philippines. This species is typically found solitary, feeding on small invertebrates and fishes. The juvenile is golden-yellow with parallel blue lines. There are two vertical dark bands in the head region and a dark spot edged blue near the base of the tail. Most notable are the trailing filaments on the dorsal fin.

Snappers tend to be excellent eaters in the aquarium and will accept almost anything, including dry food, shrimp, fish, and clams. They often appear to have endless appetites.

Squirrelfishes (Holocentridae)

The squirrelfishes with their large eyes and mouths are the "night hawks" of the coral reef, hiding during the day in caves, crevices, and under ledges. They have large eyes, stout spines on their fins, and rough scales. These predatory nocturnal fishes are found in all tropical seas and are classified into various genera. Their predominant color is red, with contrasting markings of black, white, or yellow. In the natural habitat, they are found either solitary or in small groups, depending on the species. Squirrelfish feed mainly on small invertebrates such as shrimp and crabs.

Squirrelfishes from the Indo-Pacific and the Caribbean are commonly available for aquariums. The Russet Squirrelfish *(Sargocentron rubrum)* is imported from the Pacific and Indian Oceans. The fish is predominantly red with longitudinal white bands. The fins of the Russet Squirrelfish also bear red and white markings.

The Bigeye Soldierfish *(Myripistis murdjan),* also from the Pacific and Indian Oceans, is often available. This species lives in small groups on coral reefs, finding protective cover under ledges. This fish is pink to red with darker color accents on the scales and a distinct brown bar at the edge of the gill cover.

Squirrelfishes have not gained as much popularity as many other home fishes. This is due in part to their predatory behavior and nocturnal habits. However, they adjust well to aquariums and are hardy. They are also good feeders, although newly introduced specimens may refuse certain foods. In this case, provide them with small live fish or shrimp and alternate with other foods. Squirrelfish tend to be timid in aquariums and must be provided with ample areas for refuge and protection from light that can be excessive for these nocturnal fish.

Surgeonfishes (Acanthuridae)

The surgeonfishes are among the most popular aquarium fishes. The name refers to a pair of short spines near the base of the tail. Some surgeonfishes are commonly known as tangs. When the fish is alarmed, the spines, which normally lie flat, are erected for defense. Surgeonfishes are found throughout the world's tropical seas, normally inhabiting coral reefs, patch reefs, and rocky areas, but also schooling in open water. Surgeonfishes have small teeth and small mouths. In the natural habitat, they typically graze on algae, which forms a major portion of the diet for a majority of species. In some species, juvenile color differs from adult color.

The Palette Tang (*Paracanthurus hepatus*) is an aquarium favorite that ranges from the Central Pacific to East Africa. It lives on reefs in schools, feeding on algae and small invertebrates. It is a rich blue, with a yellow tail and striking black markings on the body and fin edges. Since these tangs tend to be aggressive toward one another, ample room must be provided; otherwise, keep only one specimen in a community aquarium.

The Yellow Tang (*Zebrasoma flavescens*) is another popular Indo-Pacific fish. As its name reveals, this surgeonfish is brilliant yellow. Like other surgeonfishes, it does well in captivity provided it receives an adequate diet.

The Blue Tang (*Acanthurus coeruleus*) is a common fish of Atlantic coral reefs. Adult color differs from juvenile color. Young fish are yellow, but as they mature, color changes to gray-purple and then to blue.

The Powder-Blue Tang (*Acanthurus leucosternon*), also an Indo-Pacific species, is one of the most sought after and strikingly beautiful surgeonfishes. The fish is light powder blue, with a portion of the body white and the head black. The dorsal fin and tail are yellow. This tang, with very particular dietary needs and intolerance of poor water quality, is one of the most difficult species to maintain in captivity. It must receive abundant plant food, especially algae. It is extremely aggressive toward others of its own kind, so only one specimen should be kept per aquarium. It is not a fish for the beginning marine hobbyist.

In contrast to the Powder-Blue, the Naso Tang (*Naso lituratus*) is easier to maintain than many other surgeonfishes. The body color ranges from gray to brown-gray. The dorsal fin is yellow; there are two bright orange spots on the tail fin base. The lips are orange also. In the natural habitat, this species swims in small groups or singly. It grazes primarily on algae.

Equally hardy is the Yellow Sailfin Tang (*Zebrasoma veliferum*). This tang has extremely high vertical fins. The juvenile is yellow with brownish vertical bands on the body. This pattern changes as the fish matures. In the natural habitat, the Sailfin is found in groups. Like other tangs, it grazes on algae. This species adapts well to an aquarium and is an excellent choice for the beginner.

The majority of the surgeonfishes do well in captivity, but they must receive ample supplies of algae to grow and remain healthy. They will also eat animal foods, but these should not constitute a major part of the diet.

Triggerfishes and Filefishes (Balistidae)

The triggerfishes and filefishes are found in all tropical seas. Both are laterally compressed, have rough skin with scales in the form of small projections (spinules), or have spiny bony plates.

Triggerfish are so named because their foremost dorsal spine can be erected and then locked in position by the spine just behind it. When the second dorsal spine (the "trigger") is depressed, the first spine is released. Triggerfish normally swim with the spine lowered, but if frightened, they will find refuge in a hole or crevice and erect the spine. This makes it virtually impossible to dislodge them from the crevice. In the natural habitat, they are usually solitary.

The coloration of these fishes varies from gray or brown to the gaudiest of patterns. Triggerfish undulate their dorsal and anal fins

▼*Top left: The Maroon Clownfish* (Premnas biaculeatus). *Top Right: The Mandarinfish* (Synchiropus splendidus). *Bottom left: The Spotted Mandarin* (Synchiropus picturatus). *Bottom right: The Jackknife fish* (Equetus lanceolatus).

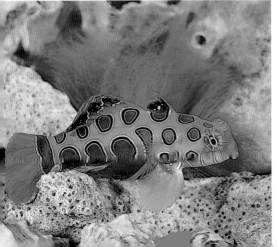

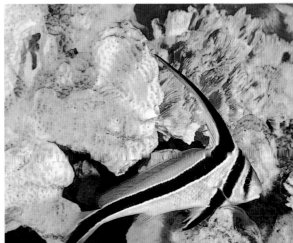

for motive power. They are inquisitive, often inspecting areas of coral, corners, and crevices.

Triggerfish are equipped with powerful teeth, which they use to crush such creatures as shrimp, crabs, lobsters, sea urchins, and mollusks.

Several species are popular as aquarium fish, the majority imported from the Indo-Pacific and the Caribbean.

The Blue-Lined Triggerfish (Pseudobalistes fuscus) is a beautiful species native to the Indo-Pacific and the Red Sea. Adult coloration differs from that of the juvenile. Juvenile fish are golden-yellow with blue lines over the body. As they mature, the body color changes to a green or burnt orange color, with the blue lines still present. This species is known to be particularly aggressive.

The most spectacular of the triggerfishes is the Clown Triggerfish (Balistoides conspicillum), a beautiful Indo-Pacific species. It is the most prized triggerfish for the aquarium. In the natural habitat, it feeds on invertebrates, including coral, and crustaceans such as crabs and shrimp. The body of the fish is bluish-black with large white ovals. There is also a reticulated yellow pattern on the fish's body. The lips are orange. This fish acclimates fairly well to the new aquarium.

The Undulated Triggerfish or Orange-Lined Triggerfish (Balistapus undulatus) is aggressive but attractive, best suited for larger aquariums. It is green-brown with curving orange lines across its body, converging toward the tail, where there is sometimes a black spot. In the natural habitat, it feeds on clams, shrimp, fish, and algae.

The Humu-Humu (Rhinecanthus aculeatus) is well-known and popular among marine hobbyists. And yes, this is the same fish mentioned in the famous Hawaiian song that tells of the "Humu humu nuku nuku apua'a" swimming by.

Small specimens do well in community aquariums and tend to be less aggressive than other triggerfish. In the natural habitat, the Humu-Humu feeds on a wide variety of foods, both plant and animal, including small fishes, invertebrates, and algae. This colorful fish is brown, with white on the underside of the body and various markings of blue, yellow, and black.

The Queen Triggerfish (Balistes vetula), a Caribbean species, is also a less aggressive species. The fish has a golden body color with a pair of curved blue stripes across the head. There are radiating lines from the eyes, which are bright blue. Long filaments are sometimes present on the caudal fin and dorsal fin. It is a beautiful species and grows rapidly in aquariums when given good environmental conditions and a balanced diet.

An aquarium fish, triggerfish cannot be considered docile. Many species are extremely aggressive toward their own species and will also chase other fish. To minimize aggression, therefore, triggerfish should not be kept with fish of about the same size. Of course, invertebrates cannot be safely kept with triggerfish.

Triggerfish are very hardy and generally adapt well to aquarium life. They fare well through the water conditioning cycle. These fish require a varied diet that should include clams, shrimp, crabs, and similar foods. They relish a live crayfish from time to time.

Filefishes are similar in appearance to triggerfishes, but their bodies are more compressed. Like the triggerfish, they also have a locking spine.

In nature, filefishes feed on coral polyps, and other small invertebrates, as well as algae; therefore, they should not be kept with any invertebrates that they can eat.

Several species are excellent aquarium fish, including the Scrawled Filefish *(Aluteres scriptus)* imported from the Philippines. In the natural habitat, it feeds on gorgonians, small worms, coral polyps, and other invertebrates, as well as algae. This fish is brownish with blue spots on the body and wavy lines on the head region. Its tail is much longer than that of other species of filefishes.

One of the most popular is the Longnosed Filefish *(Oxymonacanthus longirostris).* This beautiful fish has a greenish body with oval orange spots. Peculiarly it tends to swim with its head pointed toward the aquarium bottom. It is an excellent aquarium specimen and can be kept with several of its own species.

This species is more difficult to keep than other filefishes and it is not recommended for the beginner. Filefish should be fed plankton, shrimp, clams, and fish.

Another commonly collected fish imported from the Pacific, especially from Hawaii, is the beautiful Orange-Tailed Filefish *(Pervagor spilasoma).* It has a white to dusky body with a distribution of black spots and an orange tail fin.

Filefishes swim slowly and tend to be shy. Overly aggressive tankmates will prevent them from receiving an adequate supply of food. These docile relatives of the triggerfishes must be supplied with an ample diet that includes an abundant supply of algae.

Trunkfishes, Cowfish, and Boxfish (Ostraciidae)

Encased in a "box" of fused scales, these fish comprise one of the oddest of all marine fish groups. They include numerous species found in all tropical seas. Although not the most agile of fishes, they swim surprisingly well considering their body restriction.

When disturbed or frightened, all species of this family can discharge poisons into the water from their skin. This poison can kill other fishes including the fish itself. However, this is seldom a problem in aquariums unless the fish are unduly chased or frightened. Your fish retailer can give you additional information on how to safely maintain these interesting fishes in your aquarium.

Several species are commonly available for home aquariums. The Blue-Spotted Boxfish, *(Ostracion meleagris)* is a beautiful Indo-Pacific species. The fish's body color ranges from black to a dark blue. The upper portion of the body is black, with white spots. The lower portion of the body is blue with orange dots edged with black.

The Polka-Dot Boxfish *(Ostracion cubicus)* is a commonly imported omnivore from the Indo-Pacific. Typically, its diet in the natural habitat includes worms, crabs, other invertebrates, and algae. The juvenile and adult coloration differ. Juvenile fish are yellow with dark spots distributed over the body. As they mature, the fish become brownish with the spots becoming light in color.

The Long-Horned Cowfish *(Lactoria cornuta)* possesses distinctive spines in front of the eyes and under the tail. In nature, it is found on coral reefs, where it feeds on small invertebrates. The fish is a variable yellow color with blue markings. Commonly imported from regions of the Indo-Pacific, this slow feeder should never be kept with aggressive fish.

Trunkfishes should not be kept with members of their own species, but may not be compatible with other species. They must not be kept with fast-moving fishes that can prevent their receiving adequate food.

This family has small mouths and therefore requires small pieces of food. It will accept almost anything, including plankton, brine shrimp, algae, and small worms.

Wrasses (Labridae)

The wrasses include numerous species found throughout tropical and temperate seas. Generally elongated, their body form is diverse. As a group they are carnivorous, feeding on small invertebrates and fish. Most are very easy to keep and are compatible with most other fish. Many have the habit of burying themselves in the sand at night, or, if frightened, diving headfirst into the substrate.

The family includes many of the so-called cleaner fishes. These species clean other fish by picking off attached parasites.

The wrasses primarily use their pectoral fins to swim. During rest, many will hide behind rocks or simply lie on the bottom. Their coloration, often brilliant, generally differs between juveniles and adults and between males and females.

Because of the popularity and availability of this group of fishes, several species will be discussed. One of the more commonly available species is the beautiful Twinspot Wrasse *(Coris aygula),* highly sought after by aquarists. The juvenile is white with black spots of varying sizes on the anterior half of the body and on the dorsal fin. There are two large blotches of orange on the body and two black spots on the dorsal fin just above the orange coloration. The coloration of the adult differs. The anterior half of the body is gray to white with black spots of varying sizes, and the remainder of the body is black. A lighter vertical band is found between the white (or gray) and the black areas. These hardy and active fish do very well in aquariums and are highly recommended for any marine hobbyist.

The Clown Wrasse *(Coris gaimard),* from the Pacific and Indian Oceans, is similar in coloration in its juvenile form to the Yellow-Tail Wrasse. In the natural habitat, it is found near rocky areas and on patch reefs. The juvenile is red-orange, with five to seven white bars on the body. These bars are edged in black. It makes an excellent addition to any aquarium.

A strange-looking fish, the Bird Wrasse *(Gomphosus varius)* is equipped with a long snout used for probing holes and crevices for food. This wrasse feeds on fish, small crustaceans, and other invertebrates. The male is green and the female is brown. The Bird Wrasse is also popular for marine aquariums.

The Yellow-Tail Wrasse *(Coris formosa)* is a frequently imported Indo-Pacific species. Juvenile fish are red-orange with three white, dark-edged vertical body bands, much like the juvenile Clown Wrasse. There are also two white areas on the head region. As the fish matures, the color changes, with a loss of the bands, the body becoming a uniform dark color.

The Eclipse Hogfish *(Bodianus mesothorax)* feeds on small invertebrates and fish on the Pacific coral reefs. A popular and hardy species, this fish is suitable for the beginner. Juvenile and adult coloration differ. The adult is brown anteriorly; the remainder of the body is yellow.

The Bluehead *(Thalassoma bifasciatum)* is a commonly sold Caribbean wrasse. In the wild, the juvenile fish is known to clean parasites from the body of other fish. Juvenile coloration of the Bluehead differs from that of the adult; male coloration differs from that of the female. The males have a deep blue head and a green body. The females are yellow with longitudinal dark bands along the body. The juvenile fish of this species are similar in color to the adult females.

The wrasses thrive in aquariums. They are active, feed well on most food offered, and tolerate a variety of conditions. They are highly recommended to the new aquarist. It is important to provide an ample depth of fine substrate in an area of the aquarium, since some species like to bury themselves in the sand at night. This is a behavior that is quite common among this group. In fact, when some wrasses are introduced into an aquarium, they may bury themselves for several days before swimming out in the open.

Chapter Six

Selecting Marine Invertebrates

In addition to the variety of available coral reef fishes, there are even more numerous species of invertebrates that make interesting additions to any home aquarium. However, as indicated in the preceding section on fishes, many invertebrates are not compatible with some species of fishes. The major dietary items of many fishes include small invertebrates; therefore, you must select carefully when combining invertebrates and fish. In addition, to complicate matters, many invertebrates are not compatible with other invertebrates, so the selection of invertebrates for the community aquarium is also of paramount importance.

◄ *Top left: A beautiful soft coral with opened polyps. Top right: This soft coral (Dendlonepthya sp.) is fairly common in marine aquariums. Center left: The Orange Tube coral* (Tubastrea faulkneri). *Center right: Moon coral* (Goniastrea sp.). *Bottom left: Tube Anemone (Cerianthus sp.). Bottom right: One of the many species of sea anemones available for marine aquariums.*

Invertebrates make such fascinating inhabitants that marine aquariums can be set up primarily with them. However, such aquariums are best attempted after you have had successful experience keeping marine fish and several hardy invertebrates.

Invertebrates are far more sensitive than fish to changes in water quality. Invertebrates are intolerant of chronic low-dissolved oxygen levels, high nitrate, or high organics. For that reason, if you are maintaining fish and invertebrates together, and the water quality begins to deteriorate, you will usually see behavior changes in the invertebrates long before you observe such changes in the fish.

Another disadvantage in maintaining invertebrates with fish should be pointed out: Invertebrates are very sensitive to chemicals typically used to treat fish diseases, should it become necessary to treat your fish, transfer the invertebrates to another aquarium. Never add medications directly to aquariums with invertebrates.

Purchasing Invertebrates for the Aquarium

As with fishes, you must exercise caution in selecting marine invertebrates for your aquarium. Selecting healthy invertebrates can be far more difficult than selecting fish, but there are signs indicating whether the invertebrates are in good health.

Tropical fish stores usually stock a wide variety of invertebrates. Always take time to observe the animals before you make a selection.

• Crustaceans such as crabs, shrimp, and lobsters should be active and have bright colors.

• Sea urchins should not have lost spines or appear to be losing spines.

• Sea anemones should have well-expanded tentacles, never contracted or shriveled.

• Starfish with discolored areas on the arms should not be purchased, as this could indicate a bacterial infection.

• Brittlestars should not be purchased if they have broken arms or discolored or white patches on the body.

Differences between unhealthy (left) and healthy invertebrates can be observed easily. Sea anemones in poor health have shrunken tentacles; sea stars can have swollen areas on the arms, and sea urchins lose spines.

Acclimating New Invertebrates

Acclimating invertebrates to your aquarium should follow a procedure similar to that for acclimating new fish (see Introducing New Fish into Your Aquarium, page 49). Simply float the plastic bags with the invertebrates in the aquarium and follow the transfer procedure.

Aquariums with Fish and Invertebrates

In fish and invertebrate community aquariums, the rule for populating the fish tank holds true—minimize territorial disputes. The additional issue when adding invertebrates is the compatibility of the fish with the invertebrates. Various invertebrates are primary food sources for many fishes; for example, triggerfish feed on invertebrates, especially crustaceans such as shrimp, crabs, and lobsters. The life span of a small shrimp or crab added to an aquarium with triggerfish will therefore be short. The best approach is first to make a list of fish you would like to have in the aquarium, then a list of a few invertebrates, and then to check compatibility.

A Survey of Marine Invertebrates

There are many species of invertebrates suitable for marine aquariums. The major groups of invertebrates will be covered in the following paragraphs, with selective examples of commonly available species.

Corals, Sea Anemones, Jellyfish (Cnidarians)

A major characteristic of this large group of invertebrates is the presence of nematocysts, or stinging cells, used to immobilize prey. These primitive animals are generally sessile (attached to the bottom), while others, like the jellyfish, move freely. Corals and sea anemones are the most popular invertebrates among aquarists; they are sometimes referred to as the "flowerlike" animals of the sea. The central mouth of these invertebrates is encircled by numerous tentacles equipped with stinging cells. When a fish or invertebrate comes into contact with the tentacles, the prey is stung, trans-ported to the mouth by the action of the tentacles, and digested into the body cavity. Jellyfish are seldom kept in aquariums and will not be discussed in this section.

Corals: Maintaining corals in aquariums used to be an almost impossible task, but breakthroughs in recent years have contributed an enormous amount of information that has allowed aquarists to successfully keep many species of corals in the marine aquarium. The popularity of reef aquariums has helped stimulate interest and research to learn more about the requirements needed to successfully maintain corals. There are many species that can be maintained successfully in aquariums when provided with the correct conditions. Some species are also easily propagated.

Corals are divided into those that secrete an external calcified skeleton, such as stony corals, and those without skeletons, such as soft corals. Some species of corals are solitary, while the majority of others are colonial in growth habit. There are numerous species of stony corals. Many species within this group are responsible for the massive growths of coral reefs, including the Elkhorn Coral and Staghorn Coral (*Acropora* sp.)

Various species can be successfully maintained in the aquarium. One of these is the Flower Pot Coral (*Goniopora* sp.). It is characterized by large polyps and is represented by various species. These do fairly well, but some species have better longevity records than others. The Elegans Coral *(Catalaphyllia jardinei)* is a beautiful species with tubular tentacles. The coloration is typically green with pink tips, although there are color variations. This coral is popular due to its appearance and its hardiness in the aquariums. The Clove Polyp (*Clavularia* sp.) is a beautiful and hardy species. It is characterized by solitary polyps emerging from a stolon. The polyps are large with featherlike tentacles. This coral, like many others, seldom requires supplementary feedings.

A hardy Caribbean coral is the Rose Coral *(Manicina areolata).* In the natural habitat, it is usually found in areas of high sediments and tends not to be as sensitive to environmental water fluctuations as other corals. It is a solitary species. Another representative species is the Mushroom Coral (*Fungia* sp.) with its disk-shaped appearance. It requires bright light and does fairly well in aquariums.

The soft corals include gorgonia and sea whips. These corals lack an external calcareous skeleton. Their structural support is derived from small spicules in their tissues. Some well-known and commonly available species for aquariums are *Sarcophyton* sp. and the feathery *Xenia* sp., both from the Indo-Pacific. Unlike many stony corals, which feed only at night, these species open their tentacles to feed during daylight.

In addition to the stony and soft corals, another group of cnidarians are popular invertebrates for the miniature reef aquarium. They are referred to as corallimorphs. They look like coral but lack a calcareous skeleton and often lack tentacles. They are actually closely related to sea anemones. A well-known species is the Leather Coral (*Actinodiscus* sp.).

Maintaining corals in an aquarium is somewhat of a challenge to the new aquarist, although not impossible due to advances in understanding their requirements. They are sensitive to water conditions and must have high dissolved oxygen concentrations, bright illumination, low nitrate, ample supplies of essential trace elements like strontium, and increased water movement. They also require a good supply of calcium for proper growth.

Corals require ample illumination with the correct intensity and spectrum of light. The latter is not difficult to accomplish with the numerous types of bulbs available on the market for use with miniature reef aquariums. Proper lighting is critical, since many corals contain algae in their tissues. These algae, known as zooxanthellae, have a symbiotic relationship with the coral. The association serves both the coral and the algae. It is believed that the algae benefit by being protected in the coral tissue and by receiving a supply of nutrients from the coral. The coral benefits by using as food some biochemical products of the photosynthetic activities of the algae.

In the aquarium, some corals should be provided small particulate foods as well as live foods such as newly hatched brine shrimp. Many species do not require any supplementary feeding at all because they derive all of their nourishment from the by-products of the zooxanthellae activities.

Sea Anemones: These are hardy and one of the most suitable cnidarians for the marine aquarium. They are easier to maintain than most corals and make an excellent choice for the beginner. Sea anemones range in color from pink, green, or white to purple. They resemble corals but lack the hard outer calcium skeleton. Like corals, many species have zooxanthellae in their tissues. Though many of the popular aquarium species are solitary, numerous species occur as colonies.

Sea anemones attach to the substrate by an organ called a basal disk. This disk enables the animals to creep along the bottom until they find an area in which they will reside. The long tentacles are equipped with stinging cells that paralyze prey.

The Carpet Anemone (*Stoichactis* sp.) from the Pacific is frequently purchased to maintain with clownfish, which normally associate with this sea anemone in the natural habitat.

The Florida Sea Anemone *(Condylactis gigantea),* from the Caribbean is an attractive and hardy anemone for the aquarium. It grows large in the natural habitat. The anemone is white or dusky, with the tentacle tips either purple or yellow.

Sea anemones require high water quality and good water circulation to survive in an aquarium. Although they prefer good water movement, they should be kept away from filter intakes, air stones, and areas of strong water currents. Ample water movement assists in providing high dissolved oxygen concentrations as well as helps in dislodging the mucus that anemones naturally secrete.

Sea anemones do not always remain attached to one particular rock or portion of the aquarium. They are known to move to find a suitable attachment area. Once the sea anemone is attached to either a rock or glass, it is best not to remove it unless absolutely necessary, as it is possible to damage the basal disk.

Feeding these animals is not difficult and should be done once or twice per week, or more often if the anemone appears to shrink or the tentacles appear to wither. Small pieces of fish or shrimp should be placed directly on the tentacles.

Sea anemones must be carefully watched, especially after they are first introduced into the aquarium. If the anemone begins to shrivel or change color, it could indicate that the animal is dying. Dead sea anemones can quickly pollute an aquarium, killing other invertebrates and fish. If you suspect that the anemone is dying, do not risk leaving it in your main aquarium; place it in a quarantine tank for observation.

Tube Worms (Annelida)

Tube worms, found on all coral reefs, are members of a large group of segmented annelid worms

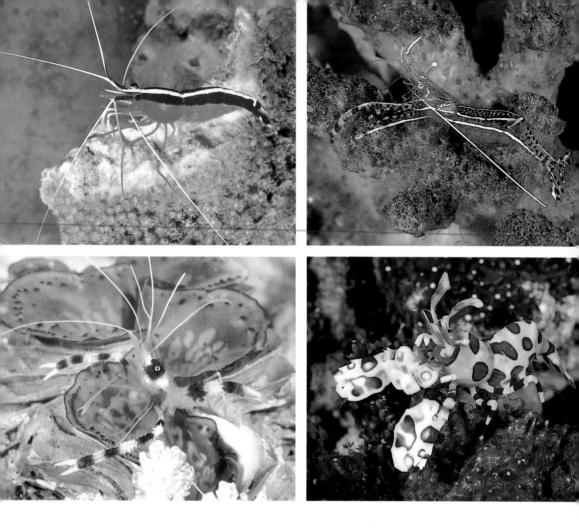

▲ *Top left: The Banded Coral Shrimp* (Stenopus hispidus). *Top right: The spectacular Harlequin Shrimp* (Hymenocera picta). *Bottom left: The Blue Lobster* (Panulirus versicolor). *Bottom right: The Red Reef Lobster* (Enoplometopus holthuisi) *from the Indo-Pacific.*

(Annelida). They are conspicuous invertebrates belonging to the class Polychaeta. These sedentary worms are characterized by their ability to construct tubes using a variety of materials, including secreted mucus, sand grains, shell bits, or calcium. The worms that inhabit the tubes have a feathery crown of tentacles that varies in color from yellow or orange to red. These specialized tentacles serve a dual purpose: for respiration and for a trap to capture small food particles. When startled, these worms rapidly contract the tentacles into the safety of their tubes. The tube worms are subdivided into two groups, the Sabellid and the Serpulid worms.

The Sabellid worms secrete soft flexible tubes that incorporate fine bits of sediment, sand, and other materials. Their crown of tentacles is quite large and often very colorful. The tubes can be more than 6 inches (15 cm) in length, each with a protective closure called an operculum, which closes off the tube once the worm has retracted its tentacles. A readily available species is the tube worm *Sabellastarte magnifica* from the Caribbean. It has maroon and white tentacles. A tube worm similar in coloration, imported from the Pacific, is *Sabellastarte indica,* probably the most common species found in tropical fish stores.

The Serpulids secrete more rigid limestone tubes that form spirals. These limestone tubes can be found over rocky substrates and on coral rock surfaces. These worms are also very colorful, the crown of tentacles being yellow, white, red, or blue. In this group of worms, depending on the species, the tentacles are often arranged in whorls like a corkscrew. The most common species on coral reefs is *Spirobranchus giganteus,* sometimes referred to as Christmas Tree Worms. Serpulid worms are introduced to the aquarium with small pieces of coral or encrusted pieces of coral rock. Coral rock in which numerous small organisms have established themselves is often sold for aquariums as "living rock."

These rocks have a diversity of marine life growing on them, including tube worms, algae, and sponges.

With adequate food, all tube worms do fairly well in aquariums. As filter feeders, they require ample supplies of minute food particles. Liquid invertebrate foods or live baby brine shrimp are recommended.

These worms should be fed several times a day with a fine suspension of food particles, such as ground plankton, flake foods, or special commercial invertebrate foods. The safest way to feed the worms without polluting your aquarium is to use a small eyedropper to release some of the diluted suspension near the worm. If a filter return is directed to the area of the worms, you can simply place a small amount of suspension in the water flow. The water movement will then carry the particles to the worms.

Certain fish are incompatible with tube worms. Mandarin fish, blennies, filefish, pufferfish, triggerfish, and wrasses will readily seek out and eat the worms. Tube worms are incompatible with invertebrates such as banded coral shrimp, arrow crabs, and other crustaceans.

Crabs, Shrimp, Lobsters (Crustacea)

The arthropods are distinguished by their segmented body, jointed legs, and chitinous exoskeleton. The Crustacea, a class of arthropods, are further characterized by antennae and compound eyes. In order to grow, crustaceans must periodically molt their old shells. Crustaceans, especially crabs and shrimp, are a popular group of invertebrates for marine aquariums. As a group, they are interesting, hardy, and readily available.

The crabs are distinguished by their dorsoventral (top-to-bottom) flattening and rounded bodies. They also possess claws that can be quite large. The other appendages are adapted to the crabs' existence as bottom-dwellers; some crabs have rear legs modified into paddles for swimming. Numerous species of crabs are recommended for the marine aquarium, some of the most popular being hermit crabs, arrow crabs, sponge crabs, and boxer crabs. Other species of predatory crabs, especially swimming crabs or those with large claws, are not suitable for aquariums.

Hermit Crabs occupy the shells of abandoned snails, which afford them protection from predators. The abdomen of these crabs, unlike that of other species, is unprotected by a shell of chitin. As they grow, hermits must find increasingly larger snail shells to accommodate their bodies.

Hermit crabs are found worldwide, including in the Indo-Pacific and the Caribbean. They are variable in color and can be red, brown, or blue. Some species have claws of equal size, while others, such as *Pagurus* spp. have one claw larger than the other.

Some species, such as *Dardanus pedunculatus,* have a habit of attaching anemones to their borrowed shells. When these hermits require a new shell, they will transfer these anemones to it. It is fascinating to observe how the hermit repeatedly touches the anemone on the old shell with its claws. The anemone will release the holdfast, allowing the hermit crab to move the anemone to the new shell.

Hermit crabs are among the easiest of all crabs to maintain in an aquarium. They are always actively dragging their shells across the bottom looking for food. When frightened, they quickly withdraw into their protective shells. Limit the number of hermit crabs to one or two in less than 20 gallons (75.6 L) of aquarium water. The crabs should be approximately the same size to prevent the larger crab from attempting to dislodge the other from its shell. Since hermit crabs can grow quickly, they must have an ample supply of empty shells. It is amusing to watch these crabs try on different shells to find the best fit.

Hermits make excellent additions to community aquariums and are compatible with a majority of fish. Very large hermits should be avoided, as they are capable of attacking some smaller fish. As scavengers, they will eat almost anything offered, including pieces of shrimp, clam, fish, or dry foods. Some species have an appetite for algae.

Arrow Crabs *(Stenorhychus seticornis)* are a popular species from the Caribbean. They are spiderlike in appearance, with long thin legs, large eyes, a pointed rostrum with small projections, and small claws. These agile invertebrates move over rocks and pieces of coral as they feed.

These interesting crabs tend as adults to be aggressive among themselves, so only one crab should be kept in an aquarium. The only exception is if you are able to obtain a mated pair.

Arrow crabs feed on various types of foods. They are compatible with nonaggressive fishes and spend a great deal of time looking for food and protecting themselves from potential enemies. They must never be kept with fishes such as triggerfishes or burrfishes, which will readily make a meal out of them.

Sponge Crabs (*Dromia* spp.) from the Caribbean are unusual little crabs that camouflage themselves with live sponges. The crabs find a sponge, trim it to size, and secure it on their backs with their hindmost legs.

These crabs will scavenge the aquarium bottom, eating bits of available food. They are extremely interesting and hardy additions to the marine aquarium.

Boxer Crabs (*Lybia* spp.) are named for their habit of carrying sea anemones in their claws as a means of defending themselves from their enemies. When approached by a potential enemy, the crabs will raise their claws with their anemones in front of them, attempting to drive off the intruder. The alternating thrust of the left and right claws resembles the motion of a boxer.

Several Indo-Pacific species are imported for home aquariums. The Boxer Crab *(Lybia tessellata)* is a colorful dusky-colored crab with black-edged orange markings on the body. These crabs are an amusing and interesting addition to any marine aquarium.

The Teddy Bear Crab *(Polydectus cupulifer)* is covered with fine yellow fuzzy strands, from which it derives its name. It also carries sea anemones in its claws. These crabs are sometimes sold without sea anemones. Such crabs introduced to an aquarium with anemones might attempt to dislodge them to carry around for protection.

These crabs have requirements similar to other crabs and should be provided with small pieces of fresh shrimp, fish, or clam.

Shrimp are some of the most colorful crustaceans for a marine aquarium and do fairly well, provided they are not kept with aggressive fishes. Coral reefs are inhabited by a large diversity of shrimp species, many of which make excellent invertebrate additions to the marine aquarium. Shrimp have cylindrical bodies, a pointed rostrum, and a fan-shaped tail fin (telson). Some species, especially those known as cleaner shrimp, have extremely long antennae. In the natural habitat, these shrimp, like cleaner fish, will remove parasites from a fish's body. A wide variety of shrimp are available, including the Banded Coral Shrimp, the Harlequin Shrimp, the Candy-Striped Shrimp, and various species of Anemone Shrimp. As with other crustaceans, ample refuge areas must be provided, especially during molting. The period after molting is the most dangerous for crustaceans, since it takes time for the new shell to harden. Without a refuge area, the newly molted invertebrate can be quickly eaten by other aquarium inhabitants.

The Banded Coral Shrimp *(Stenopus hispidus)* has always been a favorite invertebrate among marine aquarium hobbyists. It is a widely distributed species found in the tropical Atlantic, the Indo-Pacific, and the Red Sea. It typically lives under ledges and in crevices on the reef.

The body coloration is white with red bands and claws, and long white antennae. Banded Coral Shrimp are one of the "cleaner shrimps," removing parasites from fish in the natural habitat. The typical behavior of cleaner shrimp is the waving of the antennae as the shrimp rocks its body from side to side. This signals the fish, which can then approach for cleaning.

If possible, Banded Coral Shrimp should be kept in pairs in an aquarium. If a mated pair cannot be obtained, only one should be kept. Banded Coral Shrimp should not be combined with very small fishes, as the shrimp are efficient at catching them.

These shrimp are an excellent addition to the aquarium. They must be provided with ample hiding areas under rock or coral ledges. They are easy to feed and will accept various types of food. Small pieces of raw fish, clam, and even shrimp are readily accepted.

The Harlequin Shrimp *(Hymenocera picta)* is without question one of the most beautiful of all shrimp. It is native to the Indo-Pacific and in the natural habitat is found in pairs.

The coloration and patterns of the Harlequin Shrimp are truly distinctive. The body and huge flattened claws are white or pale gray with large blue or purple spots. The antennae are fan-shaped, and legs are banded in blue or purple, depending on the body coloration. The body is white or bluish, with spots and patterns edged in purple.

Since Harlequin Shrimp are very territorial, only one shrimp or a mated pair can be maintained in an aquarium. These shrimp are also carnivorous. They primarily eat living starfish, from which they saw off small morsels with their strong, sharp claws, but they are also known to eat coral or other cnidarians; thus, they are incompatible with various species of invertebrates. Their requirement for live food makes them more difficult to maintain; therefore, they are recommended only for the advanced aquarist.

The Candy-Striped Shrimp *(Lysmata grabhami)* reaches a maximum length of 2 inches (5 cm). Native to the Caribbean, it is beautiful and a frequently available invertebrate.

The dorsal portion of the body is red with a longitudinal white stripe down the middle of the back to the tail, with the ventral portion of the body yellow. The antennae of the shrimp are white and are longer than the body.

The Candy-Striped Shrimp is also one of the cleaner shrimps in the natural habitat. When kept with nonaggressive fish, these shrimp, like other cleaner shrimp, can be observed actively cleaning them.

This small shrimp is compatible with other invertebrates and with most aquarium fish. It will eat various types of foods, including pieces of clam, fish, and scallop.

Anemone Shrimp: The Ghost Shrimp *(Periclimenes pedersoni),* sometimes called the Pederson's Cleaning Shrimp, is a small tropical shrimp from the Caribbean. It lives in a symbiotic relationship with sea anemones, most commonly *Bartholomea annulata.* The shrimp is immune to the nematocysts of the sea anemone tentacles. The body of the shrimp is transparent, with white antennae, and with white and violet markings distributed over the body.

In the natural habitat, these shrimp can be found in pairs or singly, living directly on the tentacles of sea anemones. They also clean fishes of parasites. Many fish even permit the Ghost Shrimp to enter the gill cavity and mouth to remove parasites. Once the cleaning is completed, the shrimp returns to the sea anemone.

The Yucatan Anemone Shrimp *(Periclimenes yucatanicus)* is another small Caribbean species that inhabits sea anemones. It is known to be associated with the sea anemone *Condylactis gigantea.*

This shrimp is transparent, like the Ghost Shrimp, but has different body patterns. The body has white and tan saddle markings on the dorsal surface, with alternating white and purple on the legs. As in the majority of cleaner shrimp, the antennae are long and white.

Anemone Shrimp do well in aquariums and must be provided with a sea anemone. Like other shrimp, they will feed on various types of foods.

Clams, Scallops, Snails, Octopuses (Mollusks)

The mollusks are an extremely large and diverse group of invertebrates characterized by their soft bodies. The majority have external protective shells; some, however, such as the nudibranchs, squids, and octopuses, lack shells. Scientists have estimated that there are over 100,000 species of mollusks worldwide.

Clams and Scallops: The bivalve mollusks include clams and scallops. The soft body is protected by two shells held together by powerful muscles attached to the shells. Some species, such as clams, have a muscular foot that extends into the sand. The scallops are often attached to rocks, but some species are capable of moving by repeatedly opening and closing their shells. Bivalve mollusks are generally more difficult to care for compared to other mollusks. They are filter feeders and require large amounts of suspended food particles in order to flourish in marine aquariums. The scallops are more popular as

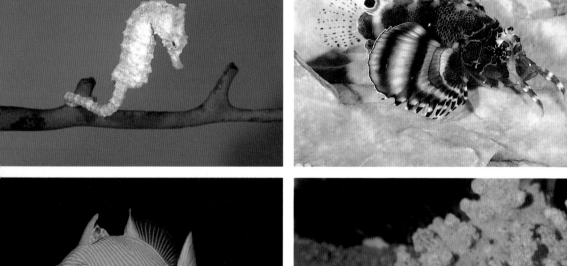

aquarium invertebrates. Clams are seldom kept, since their habit of burrowing into the substrate keeps them out of sight. In addition, many are very delicate and are prone to die quickly, causing pollution of the aquarium. The most commonly available and recommended bivalve for the aquarium is the Flame Scallop.

Flame Scallops *(Lima lima)* are frequently sold Caribbean species with a bright red mantle and protruding red or white tentacles. In the natural habitat, the Flame Scallop is found attached by thin threads to coral rock in small crevices.

The Flame Scallop must receive abundant food in order to thrive under aquarium conditions. Since it is a filter feeder, it regularly requires ample amounts of suspended food particles. This scallop can be fed with commercial invertebrate foods, or baby brine shrimp. Extreme care must be used with prepared foods, since they can readily pollute the aquarium water.

Flame scallops are not compatible with predatory snails, starfish, or certain fish, such as triggerfish or boxfish, which commonly eat mollusks.

Snails: There are far too many species of snails to discuss each

◀ *Top left: The Pantherfish* (Cromileptes altivelis). *Top right: The Square Anthias* (Pseudanthias pleurotaenia). *Center left: The Dwarf Sea Horse* (Hippocampus zosterae). *Center right: The Ocellated Scorpionfish* (Dendrochirus biocellatus). *Bottom left: The Undulated Triggerfish* (Balistapus undulatus). *Bottom right: The Russet Squirrelfish* (Sargocentron rubrum).

individual species. Various species are regularly imported for the aquarium. It will suffice to provide general information here on the care of snails in aquariums.

The familiar snails or gastropods have shells and move slowly over surfaces with a strong muscular foot. When in danger they are able to withdraw into their shells for protection. The shell surfaces of the gastropods are often beautifully marked with various patterns and colors.

Of the mollusks, the majority of snails are easy to maintain for long periods and adapt well to all aquariums. Snails can be either herbivorous, feeding on algae, or carnivorous, feeding on other invertebrates or fish. Other species of snails are scavengers, feeding on any organic materials. With very few exceptions, snails are equipped with a feeding organ called the radula. The radula is composed of small teeth that are efficient in removing food from surfaces. Herbivorous species use the radula to scrape encrusted algae off surfaces. Some carnivorous species are highly efficient as predators; the Cone Shells (*Conus* spp.), for example, have a modified radular tooth that can inject venom into the prey. Cone Shells are capable of inflicting fatal stings on humans. These species of cones are not usually available for aquariums. Other carnivorous snails include various species of the genus *Murex;* these can pull apart the shells of a bivalve using the power of their muscular foot and tip of their shell as a wedge.

Snails are compatible with most fish and invertebrates. The herbivorous species are particularly recommended to remove algae from rocks and other surfaces. The cowries are one group of the gastropods that are regularly imported for aquariums. Cowries are unusual in that their mantle covers their shell when they are active. The mantle is covered with short, white-tipped tentacles. When the cowrie is disturbed, the mantle is withdrawn into the shell. Some species feed on soft corals, hydroids, or other cnidarians, but the herbivorous species are best suited for the aquarium.

The Tiger Cowrie *(Cypraea tigris)* is a popular species native to the Indo-Pacific. The shell is white with a distribution of spots that often coalesce. The Tiger Cowrie is herbivorous, regularly grazing on algae on the aquarium glass or coral rock. It is compatible with most other invertebrates with the exception of small crabs. Crabs tend to irritate the cowrie by picking at the mantle.

The gastropods also include the nudibranchs, snails that lack protective shells. Nudibranchs are well known for their brilliant colors and distinctive patterns.

Nudibranchs: These invertebrates, also called sea slugs, are some of the most beautiful of all sea creatures. Closely related to the snails, but without shells, many are brilliantly colored and represented by numerous species worldwide. Some of the most beautiful species are in the genera *Glossodoris* and *Ceratosoma. Glossodoris festiva* is a particularly striking blue nudibranch from the Indo-Pacific. It has feathery pink and white gills and white body markings.

Nudibranchs are difficult to maintain because they are highly specialized feeders; many will accept only specific types of foods, including hydroids, sea anemones, bryozoans, or other invertebrates. Species feeding on algae are easier to maintain for longer periods. Carnivorous species must be particularly avoided, since many prey upon coral polyps, sponges, or sea anemones.

The cephalopods are the largest and most advanced of all the mollusks. These invertebrates have tentacles, and the shell is either completely lacking, as with octopuses, or reduced, as with squids. The only exception to this is the chambered nautilus, the only cephalopod with a fully developed shell. Both squids and octopuses have arms equipped with suckers.

It is virtually impossible to maintain squid in an aquarium. Most other cephalopods, such as the chambered and the paper nautilus, are equally difficult to keep. The octopus is the only cephalopod that does well—if given an aquarium of its own.

Octopuses: These have been kept successfully in marine aquariums. For the most part, their coloration ranges from dull gray to brown. Some, like the Blue-Ringed Octopus *(Hapalochlaena maculosa)* from the Pacific, are brightly colored.

This small octopus has an extremely toxic venom that is used to immobilize its prey. The venom is present in the salivary fluid and is delivered during a bite. There are several cases of human fatalities traced to bites inflicted during the handling of this octopus. Though this octopus is sometimes available in the trade, it is far too dangerous to be kept in home aquariums. Octopuses have a series of eight tentacles that surround a central mouth. The mouth is equipped with a sharp beak used to crush its prey.

Octopuses have short life spans compared to many other species of invertebrates. Tropical species are known to live less than six months. Larger species live substantially longer—more than five years.

Octopuses are highly predatory, feeding on small fish or crustaceans. They must be maintained in aquariums with a capacity of more than 55 gallons (208 L) that are devoted exclusively to them. The water quality parameters include high dissolved oxygen concentrations and low nitrite and nitrate.

Since octopuses are very shy and nervous animals, the aquarium must be decorated with sufficient rock to provide hiding areas. The aquarium must also be equipped with a tightly fitting top, since they can easily crawl out of an uncovered aquarium. Master "escape artists," they can flatten their bodies and squeeze through even the smallest openings. They will generally accept only live foods, such as fish, shrimp, and crabs. Octopuses can be trained to accept pieces of fish, scallop, shrimp, and other foods.

Octopuses are not recommended until you have been able to maintain other marine animals.

Starfish, Brittlestars, Sea Urchins, Sea Cucumbers (Echinoderms)

The Echinoderms comprise various invertebrates, including starfish, brittlestars, sea urchins, and sea cucumbers. They also include the sea lilies and feather stars, which will not be discussed in this book because of their relative unsuitability as aquarium specimens.

The word *echinoderm* refers to the spiny skin of these invertebrates, which is formed of hard plates or spines. This group of invertebrates is also characterized by nonsegmented pentamerous radially symmetrical bodies. The latter means that the body of an echinoderm can be divided into five parts around an axis.

Starfish: The most familiar of the echinoderms, they usually have five rays (arms) radiating outward from the central body disk, but there are other species that have more than five rays. Like all other echinoderms, starfish are bottom-dwellers, with mollusks their primary food. Other echinoderms, like the infamous Crown-of-Thorns Starfish (*Acanthaster plancii*), feed on coral polyps and have been responsible for the destruction of coral reefs in the Pacific.

Starfish are not difficult to maintain in an aquarium. Several species are commonly available. The Blue Linckia *(Linckia laevigata),* an Indo-Pacific species, is one of the most popular aquarium starfish. It feeds on organic materials and detritus. Although popular, it is not as hardy as many other available species, such as the Caribbean Starfish *Astropecten* sp.

Starfish are compatible with most fishes. They will survive on pieces of clam, mussel, scallop, or fish. They are not compatible with bivalve mollusks or sea urchins, which they will devour.

Brittlestars: These are a less familiar group of echinoderms. Like starfish, they have five rays radiating from the circular body disk, but they differ in that the rays are slender, long, and flexible. Many species have numerous spines on the dorsal surface of the rays. Brittlestars are normally found in the natural habitat under rocks, at the base of sponges, or in areas of heavy detritus, where they feed on organic materials.

Brittlestars, also known as Serpent Stars, are quite hardy aquarium specimens. Many species are dull in color, but some species are red or orange. Brittlestars frequently hide under rocks or corals and are seldom seen in the open areas of the aquarium. A commonly available species that lives in sponges and on gorgonians is the Spiny Brittlestar *(Ophiothrix suensoni).* It is brown, with numerous long spines on the dorsal surface of the arms. Brittlestars feed on organic materials and some are capable of capturing small prey.

Sea Urchins: These are memorable to those who have ever accidentally touched the sharp spines of any of several species in this group. Other species of sea urchins have shorter spines or thicker blunt spines. As with other echinoderms, locomotion is accomplished with numerous tube feet that enable them to move across the bottom. On the ventral surface, they have sharp teeth used to scrape algae.

Sea urchins are sometimes maintained in aquariums but do poorly unless water quality conditions are excellent. They must be supplied with ample amounts of algae on which to graze, as they are primarily herbivorous. Without a supply of algae, they will die within several weeks.

Various species are available for the home aquarium, including the fairly hardy Pencil Urchin *(Eucidaris tribuloides)* from the Caribbean. Sharp-spined urchins like the Long-Spined Urchin *(Diadema antillarum)* and the Blue-Spotted Urchin *(Astropyga radiata)* are also available as small specimens. Handle sharp-spined urchins with care; the spines can easily puncture the skin.

Sea urchins should never be introduced to a new aquarium until the aquarium has completed the conditioning period. These spiny invertebrates should not be kept with starfish or fish such as triggerfish, which will readily prey on them.

If a sea urchin begins to shed its spines or it begins to droop, it is an indication that it is dying. Promptly remove it to prevent polluting the aquarium water.

Sea Cucumbers: Sea cucumbers have soft flexible bodies. In the natural habitat, many species can be found on sand bottoms, where they feed on various organic materials. Others have evolved specialized tube feet that act as tentacles for gathering food.

Sea cucumbers are seldom maintained in marine aquariums. They are more for the curious; most sea cucumbers are not particularly attractive for several reasons: A few species have the habit of discharging their viscera into the water when disturbed; other species can secrete poisonous slime into the water that is capable of killing the aquarium inhabitants.

One species that is colorful and interesting, and does well, is the Sea Apple *(Pseudocolochirus violaceus)*. It is equipped with featherlike tentacles that are used for feeding on suspended food particles.

▼*The Naso Tang* (Naso lituratus) *is much easier to care for than other species of surgeonfish.*

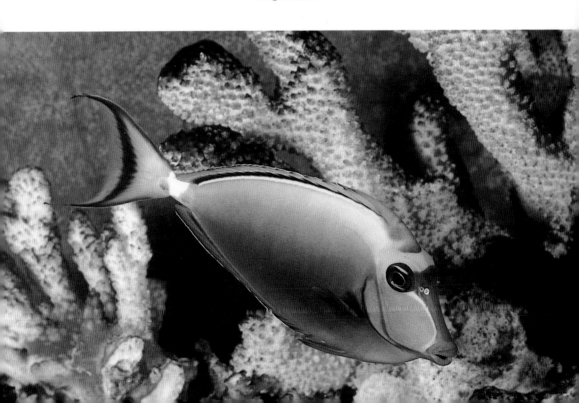

Chapter Seven
The Aquarium Conditioning Period

The importance of maintaining water quality and proper filtration was discussed at length in previous chapters. It was noted that once marine animals are placed in a new aquarium, significant changes in the water chemistry occur within a short period. These chemical changes, the most serious being elevated ammonia concentrations, can be detrimental to the newly introduced marine fish and invertebrates. The rapid accumulation of ammonia, as well as nitrite and nitrate in a new aquarium, is directly related to the establishment of the biological filter bacteria through the nitrogen cycle. Since there are insufficient numbers of bacteria in the new aquarium filter bed, several weeks or more will be required in order for the bacteria to multiply to numbers that can safely remove toxic chemicals from the water.

Some hobbyists take for granted aquarium water purification through the biological filtration process. An

◀ The Yellowtail Blue Damsel (Chrysiptera sp.).

understanding of how a biological filter bed is established with nitrifying bacteria, the conditions required for their growth and conditioning, and their effect on water quality was virtually unknown prior to the research conducted in Japan in the 1960s. The results of work by various scientists were a major milestone in the characterization and understanding of the water quality changes in new and established aquariums. As a result of the research, there was a better understanding of the chemical changes in the aquarium water as well as how to control and monitor the process to minimize the death of fish or invertebrates in a new aquarium. This research also explained why aquatic organisms died so quickly during the first few weeks in an aquarium.

Before these studies, the cause of death of newly introduced aquarium fish and invertebrates was often unknown. It was so difficult to maintain fish and invertebrates that few hobbyists were successful in keeping them alive for more than several weeks or months. In the major marine aquarium books published in the late 1950s and early 1960s, fish deaths occurring during the first few days or weeks were attributed either to water pollution or fish disease.

The process in which various types of bacteria grow rapidly over several weeks or months in a new aquarium, making the aquarium safe for maintaining marine life, is known as the "conditioning period." It is sometimes referred to as a "run-in period." The conditioning process is complex, involving various types of bacteria; however, the process can be presented simply by way of introduction.

During the conditioning period the aquarium filter bacteria increase, utilizing higher and higher concentrations of waste products from the aquarium animals. The waste products are toxic to aquatic animals, but are rendered less toxic through a series of biochemical conversions through the nitrogen cycle.

The Nitrogen Cycle

A brief overview of the nitrogen cycle was presented in an earlier section (see page 30). The nitrogen cycle is a chemical process by which nitrogen is converted through various chemical processes into chemical compounds utilized by plants and animals. The process occurs in soil and in water. Only important aspects of the cycle as they pertain to a marine aquarium will be discussed here. The emphasis here will also be the sequence as it applies to the conditioning process in new aquariums.

Ammonification

When food is added to the aquarium, it is utilized by the fish and invertebrates as an energy source for growth and maintenance. The waste products excreted into the water consist of various nitrogen products. In aquariums the principal excretory compounds are ammonia and, to a lesser degree, urea. Any uneaten food on the aquarium bottom will be utilized as food by groups of specific bacteria. These bacteria will transform such organic materials into various compounds, including ammonia. This ammonia-producing process of decay is termed ammonification. To summarize, the accumulation of ammonia in the aquarium results from a combination of direct excretory products and from the decay of nitrogen-containing products such as fish food.

As previously pointed out, ammonia is toxic to fish and invertebrates. During the conditioning period, when the aquarium is first set up with fish, ammonia will begin to accumulate. In a fully conditioned and balanced aquarium system, the ammonia produced will be rapidly detoxified by the other types of filter bacteria called nitrifying bacteria. Until the nitrifying bacteria can attain sufficient numbers to detoxify the ammonia, the water must be monitored with a test kit to assure that the ammonia is not reaching a concentration risky to the introduced fish.

Nitrification

The next step of the process is nitrification, the part of the cycle that is controlled by two principal groups of nitrifying bacteria, *Nitrosomonas* and *Nitrobacter.* The bacteria occur on aquarium surfaces such as rock, coral, and glass, but they are most densely concentrated in the substrate. Both types of these bacteria are aerobic, meaning they require high concentrations of oxygen to function and grow. In a sequence of biochemical conversions, the bacteria convert ammonia to nitrite and nitrite to nitrate.

The *Nitrosomonas* bacteria convert ammonia to a less toxic nitrogen product, nitrite. Nitrite is also toxic to marine fish, but far less toxic than ammonia. The *Nitrobacter* bacteria then utilize nitrite as an energy source and convert this to a less toxic product, nitrate.

Denitrification

The denitrification process is a chemical process that is essentially the reverse of nitrification. Nitrate is chemically reduced to ammonia and then to nitrogen gas. The process requires a different type of bacteria called anaerobes. These bacteria do not require oxygen. Since the marine aquarium is typically characterized by high concentrations of dissolved oxygen, the denitrification process is not carried out to any great extent in conventional aquarium systems. As a result, established aquariums will accumulate large concentrations of nitrate.

Conditioning Your New Aquarium

Having covered the basics of the nitrogen cycle, it should be apparent that the conditioning period is a critical time for establishment of a balanced system with a proper functioning of the biological filter.

Conditioning typically requires three to six weeks, depending on the aquarium conditions and temperature. During this time, a series of changes in the chemical composition of the water will become readily apparent. The process begins after the introduction of some fish or other marine animals that bring into a new aquarium the initial numbers of filter bed bacteria.

Features of the Conditioning Period

It is very important that only a few hardy fish be added to the aquarium to begin the conditioning of the biological filter. Not all species of fish are capable of tolerating the chemical changes that occur in the water during the conditioning period. In addition, the number of fish must also be minimal to prevent the accumulation of harmful concentrations of ammonia, especially during the early stages of the process.

The number of fish added to the aquarium should be limited to two or three. You must resist the temptation to add large numbers of fish after the aquarium is first set up in order to prevent unnecessary fish deaths. You should add any additional fish only after the aquarium has been fully conditioned.

The most commonly selected fish for conditioning the new aquarium are damselfishes. Unlike the majority of other fish species, damselfishes can withstand the chemical changes of the water during the process better than most other species. Damselfishes are not the only fish that can be added, but they will tolerate the process better than many other species. An indication of ammonia or nitrite poisoning includes increased respiration, lack of feeding, or loss of color.

The most noticeable chemical changes that occur in aquarium water quality during the conditioning period include:

- an accumulation of ammonia
- an increase in nitrite
- a steady increase of nitrate
- a decrease in pH
- an increase in organics.

The first noticeable sign of the conditioning process is the accumulation of ammonia. This will occur within a few days. The ammonia concentration will usually peak within 7 to 14 days, depending on the aquarium conditions, including temperature. The accumulation is caused by the lack of sufficient numbers of *Nitrosomonas* to completely detoxify the ammonia added to the aquarium water. The concentration of ammonia will continue until these bacteria multiply to sufficient numbers to completely detoxify the

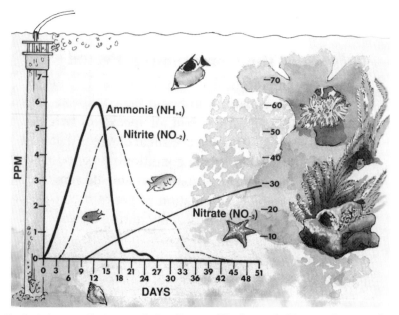

Typical changes that occur during the conditioning period in a marine aquarium.

▲*The Yellow Tang* (Zebrasoma flavescens) *fares well in aquariums, but only if provided with an adequate amount of algae and plant materials.*

ammonia being added to the water. This point in the process will be signaled by an abrupt drop in the ammonia concentration. This indicates that the *Nitrosomonas* bacteria population has increased to a level adequate to detoxify all ammonia added to the water with the existing population of fish.

The next feature of the process is the accumulation of nitrite and its conversion to nitrate. The appearance of nitrate indicates that the *Nitrobacter* bacteria have started to convert nitrite to nitrate. The nitrite will continue to accumulate until a sufficient population of *Nitrobacter* bacteria can convert all the nitrite accumulating in the aquarium water. Eventually, the nitrite concentration will peak, then

drop abruptly. This signals the end of the conditioning period. After this point, the accumulation of nitrate will continue to build up in the water at a steady rate. The only way to reduce nitrate is to make water changes and to allow the growth of algae. Maintaining low nitrate levels will be discussed later in this chapter.

Speeding Up the Conditioning Period

As discussed earlier, the conditioning period typically requires 3 to 6 weeks. It is possible to reduce conditioning time by following a few additional recommendations. The process of adding a new fish and waiting is the simplest procedure for safely conditioning a new aquarium. The major disadvantage is that it can take over a month, depending on the conditions. This time can be reduced by either: 1) seeding the aquarium with gravel from another aquarium; or 2) using specialized bacteria solutions prepared for use in aquariums.

Seeding the Filter Bed

The addition of some gravel, dolomite, or crushed coral from an already established filter bed has become a relatively common practice. A portion of substrate—several cupfuls to several pounds—taken from an established aquarium is added to the new aquarium. The marine fish are then added as described previously (see page 49). The advantage of seeding the filter bed is that much larger numbers of bacteria are added to the new aquarium. This accelerates the conditioning process and can reduce it by a week to ten days.

If you decide to use this method, make sure that the added substrate is from a fully established and disease-free aquarium. This extra precaution minimizes the chances of introducing parasites to the new aquarium.

Using Commercial Filter Bacterial Products

There are commercially available freeze-dried (lyophilized) and liquid solutions that will reduce, but not eliminate, the conditioning process. These products are essentially concentrates of nitrifying bacteria and/or various other species of bacteria; however, the freeze-dried products have not performed well and are not marketed as much as the liquid versions. The liquid products containing filter bacteria have had increased success in helping to condition an aquarium.

The earlier versions of liquid products also did not perform as well as anticipated. The major complaint was an exceedingly long lag time before the nitrite dropped to safe concentrations. Newer formulations have been significantly improved and will reduce the conditioning period. There are many types of these products being marketed, and not all have a good success rate. You should check with your aquarium store to learn which ones perform the best for reducing the conditioning period.

Monitoring the Aquarium

It is critical to monitor the aquarium water during the conditioning process. Ammonia, nitrite, nitrate, and pH kits are essential to track progress and to confirm that conditioning is proceeding normally. Since the bacteria are sensitive to varying aquarium conditions, monitoring assures that changes can be implemented if necessary.

A pH test should be performed every few days to ensure that the pH of the water is within the acceptable 8.0 to 8.3 range. When synthetic seawater is first mixed, the initial pH will usually be within the range of 8.0 to 8.5; however, after the conditioning process, you may notice a reduction in the pH. This is perfectly normal. Do not allow the pH to drop below the stated acceptable pH range, since nitrification can be adversely affected at low pH.

An ammonia and nitrite test should be performed every day. The concentration of ammonia or nitrite in the water should not exceed the safe level as indicated in the test kits used. If the concentration is unsafe, a partial water change must be made using freshly mixed seawater. Daily water changes may be needed, but by initially stocking only a few hardy fish in the aquarium, this can be minimized.

Once nitrite begins to appear, a nitrite test should be performed every few days, then, once the ammonia and nitrite concentrations drop to nontoxic concentrations, the aquarium is conditioned.

It is important that no medications or other chemicals be added to the aquarium during the entire conditioning period. The sensitive filter bacteria can be inhibited by chemicals, and this can slow the conditioning process. The bacteria are affected either by reducing their growth rate or affecting other meta-bolic processes. Antibiotics such as erythromycin, when used at concentrations commonly used to treat fish diseases, can halt the bacterial process.

After the Conditioning Period

Once the aquarium has become conditioned, you can begin to safely add more fish and invertebrates. It is best to add a few over a period of time to ensure that you are not overloading the aquarium.

When adding new fish, you may notice a slight increase in ammonia for a day or so, but it should then decline to a safe level. This temporary increase is normal, but if a large number of fish are added and the ammonia persists, it can signal that you are reaching the maximum number of fish for the aquarium.

There is a limit to how many animals can be maintained in the aquarium. The maximum number that can be safely added to an aquarium is called carrying capacity. If the carrying capacity is exceeded, you will observe a chronic persistence of ammonia in the water. This can indicate that you have added too many fish to your aquarium. Either the number of aquarium inhabitants must be reduced or additional filters must be added to handle the increased animal load.

Chapter Eight
Aquarium Maintenance

When properly set up, marine aquariums require minimum maintenance; however, regular preventive checks of equipment are needed to ensure proper functioning of the entire aquatic system. Weekly and monthly maintenance tasks are required. In addition, a series of daily checks should be made, especially during the first few weeks after the first aquatic animals have been added. Routine daily inspection of the aquarium system ensures that problems can be found quickly and corrected before they place the fish and invertebrates in jeopardy.

As a safety procedure, whenever working with aquarium equipment, make sure that the apparatus is disconnected from electric outlets. Salt water is highly conductive and can transmit dangerous electric shocks. This is especially true when working on lighting elements or adding water to the aquarium.

It is also important to make sure that your hands are free of detergents or any other substance that

◀ *The Blue Reef Fish* (Chromis cyaneus).

could be toxic to the fish and invertebrates. If you need to remove an item from the aquarium, first wash your hands and arms well with clear warm water. Any products you use to clean the aquarium must also be free of detergent residues or other possibly toxic materials. It is recommended that you purchase brushes, sponges, buckets, and other items that will be used only in the maintenance of your aquarium.

Keeping a Journal

It is recommended that you keep a maintenance log covering the type of maintenance that has been done on your aquarium system. This is important for future reference and will aid in reminding you when you performed a specific maintenance check, filter repair, bulb replacement, water change, and so on. The log can be divided into major sections—Daily, Weekly, Monthly, Quarterly—as well as subdivided into water tests, filter cleaning, repairs, bulb replacements, water changes, and other relevant categories.

109

You can keep the record in a regular journal or, better yet, in a computer database or spreadsheet. There are any number of software programs on the market that can be used for storing and later accessing your data for checking. Many of these programs are very easy to use even if you are not familiar with databases. For example, Microsoft's Access Database program comes with a program that automatically generates the databases for you. All you need to do is supply a list of file fields, such as Record Number, Water Test Type, Results, Date Performed, and the program makes the input form and the database.

Daily Maintenance

A series of checks should be made every day to ensure that everything in the aquarium is functioning properly. In addition to turning on the aquarium light and feeding your fish, you should also routinely remove any food material or other debris that is visible on the substrate. You should also account for all fish and invertebrates and observe their overall condition and behavior.

Filters, Heaters, and Other Equipment

The next daily check involves the functioning of the filters, lighting, heaters, air stones, protein skimmers, and other apparatus.

Filters: The undergravel filter should be examined to ensure that the proper amount of air is flowing to operate the lift tubes. If the air flow appears diminished, it could be caused by a faulty air pump, clogging of the air line by accumulation of salts, or clogging of the air diffuser in the undergravel lift tube. Salt accumulation is not unusual in aquariums that have been in operation for several months or more. The salt can be removed by passing a fine wire down the plastic air tube in the filter to break up the salt accumulation. If this is not effective, it may be necessary to detach the filter tube assembly from the undergravel filter and soak the parts in warm water to dissolve the salt deposits.

Other filters, including an outside filter or canister filter, should be examined to ensure that they are operating properly. If you notice a diminished water flow, this indicates that the filter medium has become clogged with particulate matter and debris and requires servicing. Diminished flow could also be caused by a crimp in the hoses of the filter.

The light bulbs should be inspected for any signs of malfunction and replaced if necessary.

Heater: The aquarium heater should then be checked to make sure it is operating properly and the aquarium water temperature is within the acceptable range. A properly functioning heater keeps water temperature within the set range. A slight fluctuation is acceptable and will not harm the inhabitants. If the aquarium water is cooler than desired, adjust the heater control knob or dial accordingly. Do this gradually, following the instructions provided by the manufacturer of the heater. A safe approach is to turn the heater dial until the thermostat light just comes on, then wait several hours, check the temperature, and readjust as required.

Protein Skimmer: If your aquarium is equipped with a protein skimmer, check to see if it is operating properly. If necessary, adjust the air flow to the skimmer. Empty the organics and waste that have accumulated in the collecting vessel.

Air Stones: Finally, check to make sure that the air stones are operating properly. As with undergravel filters, air stones can become clogged over time as they accumulate dirt and salts. If you notice a decreased air flow, it may be necessary to remove the air stone and to clean it well in fresh water. A decrease in air flow can be caused by crimped air-line tubing, improperly adjusted air valves, faulty air pump, or salt accumulation.

Water Condition and Quality: The condition and quality of the water should also be examined daily. In a properly maintained aquarium, the water should be crystal clear and should smell fresh. Questionable odors could indicate the need for a water change. Water deterioration could be due to improper filtration, decaying food, or a dead fish or invertebrate.

Fish and Invertebrates

Daily inspection of the fish and invertebrates in your aquarium ensures that they are accounted for and in good health. This is best done during feeding when the majority of the fish swim in the open. If you do not readily see a certain fish, do not assume that it has died. Since the behaviors of fish differ, some may not readily come into the open. For example, squirrelfish tend to hide during the day and feed during the night, while many species of wrasses hide in the sand for long periods of time. However, most healthy fishes, including squirrels, soon adapt to the feeding schedule, whatever it may be.

If you do not see a particular fish for several days, examine the aquarium closely, as it may have died. It is also possible that it jumped out of the tank if there was an opening in the aquarium cover. This is not

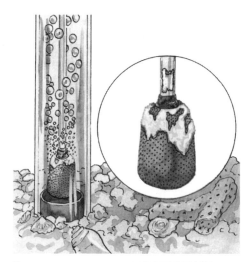

Air stones and tubing, which can become easily plugged with salt deposits and organic materials, should be periodically disassembled and washed in fresh water.

111

uncommon, especially with certain species, such as jawfish. First, look on the floor around the aquarium. If you do not find the fish, it will be necessary to move the rocks and other decorations in the aquarium to locate it. You should do this carefully and with as little disturbance as possible to the other fish and invertebrates.

In addition to checking for the presence of the aquarium inhabitants, you should note their general condition every day. You should examine the fish to see if they are behaving normally. Abnormal signs such as an increase in respiration, scratching on the aquarium bottom, or frayed fins can indicate deterioration in water quality, aggression by tankmates, or the onset of disease.

If invertebrates are maintained in the aquarium, it is also necessary to examine their condition, as invertebrates can abruptly die and rapidly pollute the aquarium, killing the other inhabitants. Check to see that anemones have their tentacles expanded and that they are attached to the substrate. Ailing anemones tend to show shrunken tentacles and may detach from the substrate. Any living corals should be examined. If any invertebrates have died, remove them promptly and follow up with an ammonia test. An ammonia test is especially important if the aquarium water is cloudy or has a peculiar odor.

Water Testing

Besides a general observation of water clarity, water tests including pH, ammonia, salinity, or any other tests should be performed as required for routine weekly maintenance. Water tests need not be performed daily except during the initial establishment of the biological filter or when new fish are added to the aquarium.

Weekly and Monthly Maintenance

Water Changes

Regular water changes are fundamentally important in any aquarium. Even though aquarium water is filtered to remove toxic components, various organic and inorganic compounds accumulate in the water over time. In fact, if an aquarium is left without any water changes, radical alterations in the chemical composition will adversely affect the aquarium inhabitants. These alterations include an increase in nitrate, decrease in pH, decrease in the buffering capacity, increase in the concentration of phosphate, increase in organic compounds, and reduction in various trace elements required by marine organisms, especially invertebrates.

▶ *Top left: The Polka-Dot Boxfish* (Ostracion meleagris). *Top right: The juvenile Yellow-Tail Wrasse* (Coris formosa) *is a frequently imported Indo-Pacific wrasse. Bottom left: The Twinspot Wrasse* (Coris aygula) *is a readily available and hardy aquarium fish. Bottom right: The juvenile Clown Wrasse* (Coris gaimard).

Increase in Nitrate: We previously noted that once an aquarium biological filter is functioning, there will be a continuous accumulation of nitrate. Even though it has generally been accepted that nitrate is not toxic, recent research suggests that high nitrate levels can interfere with the normal growth of marine fishes and have an effect on the longevity of invertebrates.

▲ *Top left: The Palette Tang* (Paracanthurus hepatus). *Top right: The Powder-blue Tang* (Acanthurus leucosternon). *Bottom left: The Orange-tailed Filefish* (Pervagor apilasoma). *Bottom right: The Clown Triggerfish* (Balistoides conspicillum).

Decrease in pH: Although several factors affect the decline of pH in aquarium water, chemical by-products of nitrification are particularly noteworthy. As previously mentioned (see page 103), the nitrification process results in an accumulation of nitrite and nitrate. However, these compounds are initially added in the form of nitrous acid and nitric acid, which eventually become nitrites and nitrates through neutralization by natural buffers. As the buffer capacity of the water (see below) is reduced, an accumulation of acids lowers the pH.

Decrease in Buffering Capacity: Natural seawater has compounds that buffer the water and maintain the appropriate alkalinity. Over time, the buffering capacity of the water lessens. The buffering compounds in the substrate eventually also become exhausted. Since synthetic sea salts contain buffers, the regular replacement of water restores any diminished buffer capacity.

Increase in Phosphate: The buildup of phosphate in aquarium water also upsets the chemical balance. Phosphates originate from the breakdown of various organic materials and accumulate regularly. Although phosphate is not toxic at concentrations normally found in aquariums, high concentrations will coat substrate particles and prevent the release of buffering chemicals. Partial water changes greatly aid in reducing phosphate.

Increase in Organics: This is another problem in marine aquariums. As discussed in The Aquarium Conditioning Period (see page 101), various filter media as well as protein skimmers will remove organics. Partial water changes also reduce the concentration of organics and the accompanying yellow color of the water. High concentrations are known to inhibit the normal growth of fish and invertebrates.

Reduction in Trace Elements: Trace elements are found in all synthetic sea salts and in natural seawater. Many trace elements are required by various marine animals for specific biological functions. For example, iodine is found in very small concentrations in seawater, but it is necessary to prevent goiter in fish. Various invertebrates accumulate large concentrations of certain trace elements, although their function is not clearly understood. The growth of macroalgae can also rapidly deplete certain trace elements. Regular water changes help restore the trace element balance in aquariums. The trace elements can also be restored using commercially available trace element solutions. These products contain needed trace elements required by aquatic organisms for normal health. A broad-spectrum trace element solution, such as CombiSan, provides trace elements for both fish and invertebrates.

As can be seen, regular partial water replacement therefore provides the numerous benefits of restoring and maintaining proper water quality. Partial water changes of 25 percent or more should be accomplished monthly. The recommended procedure is first to mix sea salt with the appropriate amount of replacement water the night before

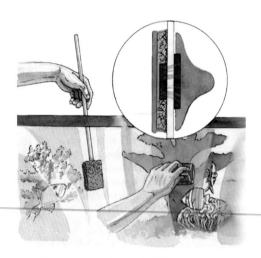

Algae can be cleaned off the aquarium glass easily using aquarium sponges or cleaning magnets.

the water change and adjust the salinity to that of the aquarium. The next day, using a siphon, remove an equivalent amount of water from the aquarium and replace with the newly mixed seawater.

Replacing Evaporated Water

It is important to replace evaporated water weekly to maintain the proper salinity and chemical balance. Tap water can be used, but in areas with extremely hard water, the continual addition of tap water can eventually cause a chemical imbalance. Under such circumstances, distilled water should be used alternately with tap water to minimize the possibility of chemical alteration of the aquarium water. It must be remembered that to destroy any chlorine or chloramines, municipal water needs to be treated with a water conditioner prior to addition to the aquarium.

Cleaning Aquarium Surfaces and Equipment

At least once weekly, all aquarium equipment should be wiped with a clean cloth. This should be done especially on areas where salt has accumulated, including the aquarium cover, hood, and sides of the aquarium. With removable aquarium covers, the easiest way to clean off collected salt and dust is to remove the cover and scrub it under warm running water.

The outside and inside glass should also be cleaned. The outside of the aquarium can be wiped with a cloth and a little glass cleaner. Be careful to use only a small amount of the cleaner and never use it on the top of the tank where it could get into the water.

The inside glass can be cleaned using various manufactured devices for removing a buildup of algae. One popular device is the cleaning magnet. Two magnets are equipped with special nonabrasive cleaning surfaces. One magnet is placed inside the aquarium and another on the outside. The magnetic force holds them in place. You simply move the outside magnet, which moves the inside magnet to remove attached algae. If the inside magnet accidentally detaches during cleaning, remove the inside magnet, rinse the cleaning surface, and inspect for any small stones. If this is not done, remaining sand or gravel will scratch the inside surface of the aquarium. This is especially important when cleaning acrylic tank surfaces, which damage easily.

Aquarium glass can also be cleaned with algae scrapers or cleaning sponges. The first device uses razor blades attached to a long handle. The movement of the cleaning head scrapes algae off the glass. The sponge type has a sponge, attached to a long handle, that will also remove algae from the glass. As with the cleaning magnets, you will avoid damage to the aquarium by frequently inspecting the cleaning head of either device to make sure small particles or stones are not trapped.

Replacing Fluorescent Bulbs

The fluorescent bulbs used in the aquarium hood have a finite life and must be replaced periodically. The bulb may still be functioning, but the intensity of the light will gradually diminish. Check with the manufacturer to find out how often to replace the bulbs. For example, if a bulb is rated for a 2,000-hour life and your aquarium is illuminated for 10 hours daily, you will need to replace the bulb approximately every seven months.

Cleaning Decorative Aquarium Items

Generally, there is little or no need to clean the various decorative items used in the marine aquarium. Algae will grow on various rocks, coral, and shells, in time giving the aquarium a more natural appearance. In addition, small invertebrates will begin colonizing these areas. From time to time, however, you may wish to clean off excessive growths of algae or accumulated dirt and sediment from coral and shells. These items can be removed, cleaned, and rinsed with a small clean toothbrush in fresh water. Never use any type of cleaning solvent or detergent to clean decorative items. These products are toxic to fish and invertebrates. Decorative items generally need to be cleaned only once every three to four months.

Cleaning Aquarium Filters

The various types of filters used in marine aquariums require maintenance to ensure performance. Depending on the filter type, maintenance needs to be done anywhere from every 3 to 12 weeks. You should follow the manufacturer's instructions for the cleaning of filters and replacement of media.

Undergravel Filters: Since these filters utilize the aquarium gravel as their filter medium, the layers of the filter bed can become laden with debris. If the filter bed becomes clogged, the filter will not function properly. Therefore, it is important to gradually stir up the top layer of the filter bed once every few weeks to dislodge particles and ensure a uniform flow of water through the filter bed. The debris that is stirred up will be removed by an outside filter.

If the undergravel filter bed is heavily laden with organic materials, use a special siphon cleaner that removes water as it cleans the top surface of the filter bed. This process can be followed once every four to six weeks or as required. The frequency is lessened when the aquarium is equipped with an additional outside filter.

Outside Filters: These filters, including canister filters, require cleaning every four to eight weeks, depending on the biological load in your aquarium. This entails removal and replacement of the activated carbon and filter floss. Always retain a portion of the old floss and add to the new floss. This ensures that some of the filter bacteria are retained in the filter. When replacing activated carbon, rinse it with tap water to remove fine dust particles prior to placement in the filter.

Water Testing

A series of water tests should be performed weekly or monthly. This assures that the water quality remains within acceptable ranges for each parameter.

A weekly pH test is mandatory for all marine aquariums. A pH test will determine if the acceptable range is within 7.8 to 8.3. For the majority of marine aquariums, especially those with invertebrates, the pH should be maintained within 8.0 to 8.3. As discussed previously, the pH will decrease over time and therefore must be monitored. If the pH has decreased, it will be necessary to make an immediate partial water change.

A salinity test should also be made weekly to ensure that salinity is within an acceptable range. If the salinity has increased, simply add enough fresh dechlorinated water to bring the salinity back to an acceptable level. As previously discussed, the salinity is determined by first testing the specific gravity using a hydrometer (see page 29).

A nitrate test should also be made weekly. The accumulation of nitrate is determined by various factors, including the initial number of fish and invertebrates in the aquarium, amount of food fed, type of filtration system, and extent of algae in the aquarium. Since algae utilize nitrogen compounds, aquariums with an abundant growth of algae will not accumulate nitrate as rapidly as those with little or no algae. Excessive concentrations of nitrate in the water, while not directly toxic, can interfere with the normal growth and longevity of marine fish and invertebrates. Invertebrates generally do not tolerate excessive concentrations of nitrate in the water.

Other tests, including those for ammonia, nitrite, and dissolved oxygen, are seldom required once the aquarium is functioning properly and has undergone the conditioning period. The only exception that would necessitate more frequent testing would be if a substantial modification is made to the aquarium system—for example, the addition of a new filter, a complete cleaning of the filter systems, a change in the type and amount of food fed, or the addition of several new fish.

Chapter Nine
Nutrition

Nutrition is a critical factor in the longevity of marine fish and invertebrates in aquariums. Since the greater majority of fish and invertebrates are caught in the wild, the aquarist faces the problem of providing foods that are good substitutes for those normally eaten in the natural habitat. The diet must include enough variety to supply the appropriate proportion of nutrients.

Satisfying the requirements of marine fish can be problematic. Many species have strict requirements for only certain types of foods. For example, sea horses will eat only live foods. Various species of butterflyfish are so selective that they will feed only on live corals. Many invertebrates, such as nudibranchs, die rapidly in aquariums without a supply of live foods. There are many species of fish and invertebrates that are so specific in their feeding habits that they should never be purchased for a home aquarium.

The beginning aquarist can sometimes be fascinated enough with the vivid colors and variety of marine fish to purchase them without considering the difficulties of keeping them alive and healthy. For example, lionfish are magnificent and very hardy in the aquarium, but they require a regular supply of live small fish as their principal food. They can be trained to eat other foods, but this could take some time. In the meantime, a supply of live fish must be kept readily available for regular feedings.

The nutritional requirements of invertebrates are less known than the requirements of marine fish. The latter information is from limited research with a small number of fish species. Though the study of marine fish nutrition is in its infancy, research to date has provided information on generalized requirements of marine fish.

Marine Fish Nutrition

The health and longevity of marine fish largely depend on the quality and quantity of the diet. The

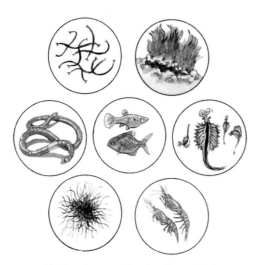

Various types of live foods can be fed to marine fish. Clockwise from top left: bloodworms, algae, brine shrimp, shrimp, tubifex worms, earthworms, and live fish (center).

nutritional needs of fish are not static, but change especially during demanding physiological periods. To ensure normal growth, structural tissue and organ integrity, reproduction, physiological function, and disease resistance, fish must have nutritionally sound diets.

To minimize deficiencies under aquarium conditions, marine fish diets must be varied; the diet can include frozen foods, live foods, and prepared dry foods. Each of these types will be examined later in this chapter.

Food furnishes usable energy for growth, tissue repair, swimming, and other essential activities. The rate at which energy is used, called the metabolic rate, is a function of various factors, including temperature, the species of fish, its body size, and its physical condition.

You must understand that water temperature is the most important factor affecting a fish's metabolic rate. This is due to the fact that a fish's body temperature is always close to the ambient water temperature. Therefore, if the aquarium water is 80°F (26.6°C), the fish's body temperature will also be close to 80°F (26.6°C). As the water temperature increases, so does the metabolism of the fish and its energy requirements.

Marine fish also have variable energy requirements depending on the species. For example, a shark that swims continuously requires a higher caloric intake than a bottom-dwelling fish such as a blenny. And most importantly, in order to maximize growth, young fish require more calories than older fish.

Feeding Behavior of Marine Fish

Marine fish species are classified as herbivores, carnivores, or omnivores. This is a generalization, since food habits can change depending on the species, the size of the fish, and the stage of its life.

Herbivores feed on plant materials almost exclusively. Marine fish such as various surgeonfish and parrotfish are classified as herbivorous. They consume large quantities of algae and other plant materials each day on the reef. Research has shown that plant materials can account for 94 percent or more of their daily diet. Such animals have evolved a long intestinal tract that allows for the longer time required to digest plant materials.

Carnivores, such as hawkfishes, gobies, eels, and sharks, prey either on other fishes, invertebrates, or both. In contrast to herbivorous fishes, carnivores have evolved a shorter intestine for digesting food.

Omnivores feed on a variety of both plant and animal materials. The great majority of coral reef fishes are classified as omnivorous. As can be expected, omnivores have developed an intestinal tract suited for the digestion of a wide variety of foodstuffs.

Dietary Requirements: A Brief Survey

The basic nutrients required by fish include proteins, lipids, carbohydrates, vitamins, and minerals. Although the exact requirements of each species are unknown, research on both freshwater and marine fish has provided basic guidelines for feeding marine aquarium fish.

Proteins

Marine fish have a requirement for abundant protein in their diet. In nature, protein comprises the largest portion of the diet. Young fish require higher protein levels than adults. If a fish diet is lower in protein than required, growth rates, tissue repair, and disease resistance are directly affected.

Proteins are found in plant and animal materials and are comprised of amino acids. The nutritional value of a particular protein is based on the types and amounts of its amino acids. Animal proteins are more complete, providing essential amino acids often absent in plant proteins. There are 25 amino acids common to all proteins, of which 10 are essential to various species of fish.

Amino acids are comprised of proteins and are divided into two categories: those that can be synthesized by a fish by chemically converting one amino acid to another, and those that must be supplied in the diet. The latter type are called essential amino acids.

With the exception of a few species, very little is known about the exact minimum requirement of amino acids needed by marine fish. From research thus far, it is recommended that fish receive a minimum of 40 to 55 percent protein (dry weight basis) in their diet, depending on the species. Herbivorous fishes have a lower protein requirement while carnivores and omnivores have a higher protein requirement.

Lipids

Lipids or fish oils are a critical portion of the diet. These nutrients are used as energy sources and are required for the synthesis of various components of the fish's body.

The active components of dietary lipids are called fatty acids, which are comprised of long chains of carbon atoms. They can be either saturated or unsaturated, depending on the chemical structure of the lipid. Fish oils are mostly unsaturated; the fats of higher vertebrates are saturated.

As with proteins, there are essential unsaturated fatty acids required by marine fish. Fish are able to synthesize some fatty acids from other fats, but certain fatty acids must be received in the diet. Marine fish need long-chained fatty acids, often found in other marine organisms.

Too much fat in the diet of marine aquarium fish can cause accumulations of fat in the internal organs. Abnormal fat deposits in organs such as the kidneys and liver can interfere with the normal structure and function of these organs. Fish with such conditions tend to be prone to disease.

Carbohydrates

This nutrient group consists of sugars and starches. Carbohydrates are utilized by being chemically converted to sugars and then absorbed as an energy source, or being stored in the tissues for later use. Carbohydrates are important because they are essential for the conversion of amino acids and fats into various other components required for normal functioning.

While carbohydrates are an important part of the diet, not all fish can utilize carbohydrates efficiently.

In contrast to various species of freshwater fish that are efficient users of carbohydrates, marine fish cannot as readily utilize carbohydrates in the diet. Therefore, for the majority of species maintained in the aquarium, carbohydrates should not constitute a large part of the diet. Herbivorous marine fishes, such as many species of parrotfishes and surgeonfishes, however, are more efficient users of carbohydrates.

An excess of carbohydrates in the diet of marine fish is known to cause liver degeneration and associated diet-related diseases.

Fiber

Fiber is the undigestible portion of a food. Most fiber in fish diets is derived from plant materials. As will be discussed later in this chapter, the majority of commercial dry foods include plant materials.

No guidelines have been developed for amounts of fiber in a fish's diet. However, it is believed that high amounts of fiber will impair the proper digestion of other nutrients in a diet, thereby reducing the nutrient intake.

Vitamins

Vitamins are required in the diets of all fish. They have a different function from that of proteins, fats, and carbohydrates, as they are not a source of energy. Vitamins act as catalysts for other chemical reactions in the fish's body.

The need for vitamins in a fish's diet is well documented by extensive research. It is known that under aquarium conditions, when fish are fed a large percentage of prepared dry foods or are not given a proper variety of foodstuffs, vitamin deficiencies can develop. As with other nutrients, the requirements for vitamins vary with the species of fish, size and age, water temperature, amount of stress in the environment, diet, and other related factors.

Vitamins are a large group and are either water-soluble or fat-soluble. The water-soluble vitamins include the B-complex group, such as riboflavin, thiamine, and pyridoxine, as well as vitamin C. Water-soluble vitamins are abundantly found in various foods, including yeast, leafy plants, algae, and cereals. The fat-soluble types are vitamins A, E, D, and K. Fat-soluble vitamins are found in various fats and oils.

Marine fish fed large quantities of prepared dry foods with little or no natural food generally require vitamin supplementation. This is primarily due to factors related to storage and the chemical instability of vitamin C and the B vitamins. One of the common problems is the presence of antimetabolites in commercially prepared foods that can inactivate or reduce the activity of vitamins. This problem is not restricted to prepared dry foods but can also occur in some fresh foods such as fresh fish. Other problems can occur with the leaching of vitamins into the water from dry or prepared foods. It is known that within a few seconds after feeding, some water-soluble vitamins can be reduced substantially. Finally, vitamins are easily lost as a result of heat exposure or the presence of other chemical compounds that reduce vitamin activity. However, recent discoveries, including the development of a new stabilized vitamin C, have partially solved the problem of vitamin depletion in prepared foods.

A marine fish that is fed a vitamin-deficient diet will utilize the stored vitamins in its body, eventually exhausting its available vitamin reserve. If the depletion continues, deficiency signs will develop. Notable signs of vitamin deficiencies include weight loss, slow growth, loss of pigmentation, blindness, and increased predisposition to infection. It should be pointed out that vitamin deficiencies can be particularly serious with very young fishes.

Minerals

Fish are capable of absorbing some minerals directly from their environment. In addition, since marine fish continually swallow small amounts of water, they are ingesting minerals beyond their minimum requirements for normal bodily functions, including hemoglobin production and bone formation. Mineral deficiency is extremely rare in marine fishes.

Iodine deficiency is the most common mineral deficiency in marine fish diets. Calcium and phosphorous are required for normal growth. Lack of these, moreover,

may cause spinal curvature and deformed skulls in fish.

Diets that have adequate fish protein are good sources of minerals.

Types of Foods for Marine Fish and Invertebrates

Various types of foods are available for marine fish and invertebrates. A good diet will include the requirements of each species. For this discussion, the types of foods are divided into live foods, fresh and frozen foods, and prepared dry foods.

Live Foods

Several live foods are readily available, including brine shrimp *(Artemia)* and tubifex worms. Other suitable live foods are white worms, earthworms, and small fish such as minnows. If you live near the ocean, you can also collect small live shrimp to feed marine aquarium fish and invertebrates.

The advantage of feeding live foods is that the animal is receiving the ideal undeteriorated natural food, unadulterated by preservatives. Certain species of fish and invertebrates will eat only live foods.

The disadvantage of some live foods is that they can be carriers of disease agents. This tends to be the case only with foods of marine origin rather than those of freshwater origin

◀ *The Blue Velvet Damsel*
(Paraglyphidodon oxyodon).

Brine Shrimp *(Artemia),* both in the newly hatched stage (nauplii) and adult form, are excellent foods for marine organisms. The nauplii are a perfect food for dwarf sea horses, pipefishes, and other small fishes, as well as for invertebrates such as feather-duster worms that capture small food particles as they pass over their tentacles. The adult brine shrimp is an excellent food for virtually all species of fish that will accept only live foods. For most fish, however, brine shrimp should be considered a supplement rather than the sole dietary item.

Live adult brine shrimp can be obtained from most pet retailers. These shrimp must be maintained in clean salt water and kept in the refrigerator. Nauplii can easily be hatched from eggs (brine shrimp cysts). This occurs within 24 to 48 hours, depending on the hatch conditions (see Appendix).

Since most brine shrimp are poor nutritionally, they should be enriched to increase their nutritional value. This is especially important when they are being used as the main portion of the diet, such as for sea horses, pipefish, and other species. Brine shrimp are filter feeders; therefore, they will eat small particles such as yeast, microalgae, egg yolk, dried Spirulina, and other materials. Dried Spirulina is particularly good. A commercial product such as Selcon is also excellent for enriching brine shrimp. The formulation is composed of desirable fats and vitamins.

Hatching Brine Shrimp

Live baby brine shrimp are excellent for feeding small fish and invertebrates. For certain fish such as dwarf sea horses, a supply of brine shrimp is essential. It is not difficult to hatch them at home using the following procedure.

1. Obtain a hatching container such as a clean 1-gallon (3.8 L) glass jar or a specially designed clear cone-shaped brine shrimp hatching container. Make sure the containers are clean. Never use containers that have previously been used for other purposes, as residues of other chemicals or detergents can interfere with proper hatching of the brine shrimp.

2. Fill the container approximately one-half to three-quarters full with freshly made synthetic seawater. The specific gravity should be within a range of 1.018 to 1.023. The pH should be within a range of 8.0 to 8.8. The temperature of the water should be maintained within 75 to 85°F (23.9 to 29.4°C) for the entire hatching procedure. At the higher end of the range, the brine shrimp will hatch faster, usually within 24 hours.

3. Add a sufficient amount of brine shrimp cysts to the hatching container. Approximately 1 to 3 teaspoons of cysts will supply an ample amount of brine shrimp. The amount added will depend on the type of cysts purchased. Brine shrimp cysts, incorrectly called brine shrimp eggs, can be readily purchased at retail pet stores.

4. Add an air stone that is attached to a good air pump and rapidly aerate the water to keep the cysts in suspension. The water should not bubble so rapidly that foam is formed on the water surface.

5. The cysts should hatch within 24 to 48 hours. To remove the newly hatched shrimp, remove the air stone. Direct a light source toward the bottom of the container. Allow the brine shrimp to congregate. They will tend to concentrate at the bottom of the container near the light source. As they congregate, you will observe a light orange mass, which are the newly hatched shrimp.

6. Carefully place a siphon into the container and siphon off the brine shrimp, taking pains not to remove too many cysts. The shrimp can then be fed to your fish or invertebrates. Store extra live brine shrimp in a small open container in your refrigerator.

7. Clean out the container completely, wash the air stone, and repeat the instructions to hatch additional brine shrimp.

The general directions for using Selcon call for adding a 1-mL portion of the material to a 5-ounce (142-g) portion of brine shrimp. In addition, add approximately ⅛ teaspoon of dried Spirulina. Allow the brine shrimp to feed on this for two hours or until they begin to take on a green color. They can then be fed to sea horses or other fish.

Tubifex Worms: These are also readily available for feeding marine fish. They are particularly relished by butterflyfishes, batfish, and blennies. These worms of freshwater origin have high nutritional value and are readily accepted by fish. They can be maintained alive for several days or longer, depending on storage conditions.

The disadvantage of these worms is that they must be consumed immediately, before they burrow into the substrate, where they could foul the aquarium water. Start with a small portion of worms, adding worms only after the previous portion has been eaten.

Tubifex worms harbor large amounts of debris, organic materials, and potentially pathogenic bacteria. They must therefore be washed very well prior to feeding to marine fish or invertebrates. After purchasing the tubifex, place them in a small bowl in a sink with a slow flow of cold water for 15 to 20 minutes, or until the water remains clear. Store in a partially covered container in the refrigerator. Every day, pour off the cloudy water and replace with new cold fresh water.

Earthworms: These are an excellent food for marine fish and invertebrates and are especially relished by certain fishes such as triggerfish, squirrelfish, hawkfish, blennies, snappers, and other predatory fishes. Earthworms have an excellent nutritional profile. They can be collected in virtually any rich soil or after a rainstorm, when they tend to collect on the ground. Earthworms can also be purchased from bait stores.

Earthworms can be fed whole or chopped into pieces just before feeding. Since earthworms ingest large amounts of soil, it is recommended that pieces of worms be rinsed well before feeding.

White Worms (Enchytraeus): These small worms are a good food supplement for small marine fish. White worms are available commercially, but they are often bred at home by aquarium hobbyists. However, as with the culture of any live food, it requires time and patience for best results.

White worms must be rinsed well prior to feeding to marine fish. As with tubifex worms, only small numbers should be fed to ensure that the worms are consumed within a reasonable time. While white worms are an excellent food, they should be considered only a supplement for marine fish.

Small Fish: To survive in an aquarium, certain fish and invertebrates must receive live prey. Among these are the various species of lionfish. Various types of fish can be fed, including live-bearers such as minnows, mollies, and others. Feeding goldfish to lionfish is not recommended. It is well-known that severe damage to the liver can occur when feeding only goldfish to lionfish. If live fish must be offered, feed a variety of freshwater species and marine species. Bait shops are good sources of small bait fish.

Fresh and Frozen Foods

More convenient and more readily available than many live foods, various fresh and frozen foods are suitable major staples of the marine fish and invertebrate diet. Fresh foods such as fish fillets, shrimp, clams, and scallops are all excellent choices for feeding young aquarium animals. Various plant materials, including spinach, lettuce, and algae, are good supplements in diets of herbivorous and omnivorous fishes.

Various frozen foods are readily available, and include brine shrimp *(Artemia),* daphnia, fish roe, shrimp, and other items. Also commercially available are formulas prepared from a variety of fresh foods and frozen into a block. There are specific formulas for feeding invertebrates and herbivorous, carnivorous, or omnivorous fishes. There are also suitable formulas for feeding invertebrates.

Fish: Fresh fish is an excellent component of the diet for marine aquarium fish and invertebrates. An ample supply of fish can be purchased, cut into smaller pieces, and frozen for later use. If prepared properly, you can then remove a portion

from the freezer, thaw the food in a small amount of warm water, and feed to the aquarium inhabitants.

Selecting the type of fresh or frozen fish is important. Generally, white, firm-flesh fish are the most suitable. These include flounder, halibut, snapper, and haddock. Avoid oily species such as salmon, mackerel, and herring, which will cause buildup of oil on the surface of the aquarium water.

Shrimp: Fresh raw shrimp is one of the best staple foods for feeding marine fish and invertebrates. It can be used for feeding small fish by cutting the shrimp into small pieces. Large chunks of shrimp will be readily taken whole by larger fish. Pieces of shrimp are also excellent for feeding sea anemones, hermit crabs, and other invertebrates.

If you use frozen shrimp, remove a portion from the freezer, allow to thaw in warm water, then remove the shell and legs. Cut into pieces of appropriate size and feed to the aquarium animals.

Scallops, Clams, and Mussels: These are also excellent dietary staples. They should be prepared by cutting into small pieces for feeding smaller animals; larger pieces can be fed to larger animals. Mussels and clams should be cleaned thoroughly to remove any sand or other foreign material that is sometimes retained by shellfish.

Plant Materials: Spinach, lettuce, algae, and other plant materials can also be fed either fresh or frozen. If fresh materials are used, they should be briefly steamed just enough to wilt the plants. This makes it easier for fish or invertebrates to consume lettuce or spinach. Frozen spinach can be used after it is thawed. Plant materials are essential dietary items for herbivorous fishes such as surgeonfishes and parrotfishes.

Prepared Dry and Freeze-Dried Foods

This group of aquarium foods is either prepared from various ingredients and then processed into flakes or pellets, or freeze-dried. The freeze dried natural foods are plankton, daphnia, tubifex worms, and bloodworms.

All dry foods must be stored properly to retain essential nutrients. Some nutrients are volatile and will be dissipated as time passes. Those most susceptible are vitamins B_{12} (riboflavin), B_6 (pyridoxine), folic acid, and vitamin C. To minimize the destruction of vitamins, keep all dry foods tightly closed when not in use. Dry foods should be protected from moisture, heat, and light. Never store dry foods on top of the aquarium or its light fixture. As a general rule, dry foods should be used within three to six months after opening. Storing dry foods in a refrigerator will further reduce the rate of nutrient destruction.

Flake Foods: The most popular prepared foods for aquarium fish, high-quality flake foods are excellent for freshwater fish, but should not be relied on as a sole diet for marine fish.

Flake foods are prepared from a complex group of ingredients that are blended into a slurry and then pumped to a specialized drum dryer. As the slurry comes into contact with the dryer, the food is rapidly baked. Large wafer-thin sheets are produced, which are then broken into flakes.

Notable advantages of flake foods are that they are convenient to feed and store, contain the major nutrients required by fishes, and are accepted by a vast majority of fish, once they have become familiar with this type of food.

To prevent overfeeding, flake foods should be fed sparingly, a small amount at a time. Since the majority of marine animals are not surface feeders, some flake food can be held underwater near a strong water current, which will moisten the food and rapidly disperse it throughout the aquarium.

Various types of dry prepared foods are available commercially for feeding marine aquarium fish.

Pellet Foods: These foods are available in two types—sinking pellets and floating pellets.

The sinking pellet is a highly compressed globule of a granular food formula that has been steamed and forced through a die. This type of pellet sinks to the aquarium bottom and rapidly hydrates and swells. As the pellets swell, various-sized fish or invertebrates feed on the food particles. Sinking pellets are excellent for bottom-dwelling fish and invertebrates. Leftover pellets can easily foul a tank, however.

Floating pellets are manufactured using high levels of pressure, heat, and moisture. In the process, the large amounts of carbohydrates used in extrusion formulas become gelatinized, trapping air within the pellet. The trapped air is responsible for the buoyancy of these low-density floating fish foods. Since high carbohydrate content is not desirable in the diets of marine fish, and most are not surface feeders, floating foods are generally not recommended. Floating foods are useless for feeding invertebrates.

Freeze-Dried Foods: These foods, such as plankton *(Euphausia),* tubifex, and bloodworms, are prepared by flash freezing live foods and then removing the moisture while frozen. This process minimizes the destruction of essential nutrients. Freeze-dried foods are easily stored and are readily accepted by marine animals. Since it takes time for freeze-dried foods to rehydrate, it is best to presoak a small amount for several minutes before feeding to your aquatic animals.

Plankton and krill are two very popular freeze-dried foods for marine fish. These small crustaceans are harvested in the cold waters of the Atlantic and Pacific. Since they are high in protein, fats, and other nutrients, they make an excellent supplement, especially for carnivorous fishes. In addition, these shrimp contain high concentrations of pigments that enhance the natural coloration of the fish.

Guidelines for Feeding Marine Fish

Proper technique for feeding must take into consideration the natural feeding habits of the fish. The question of the frequency of feeding is one of the most commonly asked questions, especially by new hobbyists. It is often recommended that marine fish be fed either once or twice a day. However, such a schedule does not take into account that marine fish in the natural habitat are constantly browsing the coral reef throughout the day. Nocturnal feeders, on the other hand, come out onto the reef at night to feed.

Contemporary thought on feeding marine fish takes into consideration the feeding behaviors in the natural habitat of the fish; therefore, the recommendation is to offer multiple small feedings throughout the day. It is also important to understand that for proper growth, young fish must receive more food than older fish. The great majority of fish sold for marine aquariums are juveniles or subadults, with greater nutritional needs than those of mature fish.

How to Feed

The most serious problems are overfeeding and underfeeding. The former is far more common than the latter. The most serious conse-quence of overfeeding is the accu-mulation of uneaten food that can decay, foul the water through the buildup of ammonia, and possibly result in the death of the fish.

Underfeeding is a problem either when fish are fed too little or when dominant fish in the aquarium con-sume the greatest amount of food. In this situation, some fish receive ample nutrition, while others are nutritionally deprived. The feeding behavior of the fish in the aquarium must therefore be considered.

Depending on the species, each type of fish has a different behavior. There are surface-feeding fish, mid-water feeders, and bottom-feeding fishes. When feeding the inhabitants of a community aquarium, ensure that each species is receiving a share of the food.

As a general rule, your aquarium fish should be fed two to four times daily. The feeding periods should be distributed throughout the day. Young fish may require more fre-quent feedings. Alternate the types of food fed each day. Include in the diet various types, such as flake foods, freeze-dried foods, and frozen foods. Always offer small amounts of food at each feeding period, adding any additional food only after the first portion has been completely consumed.

At the conclusion of the feeding period, always remove any food that remains uneaten on the bottom to prevent decay that can pollute the aquarium water. This is especially important when feeding frozen and fresh foods such as clams, mussels, and shrimp, which can rapidly pol-lute the aquarium.

Problem Fish

It is inevitable that some fish will be reluctant to feed, especially if they have been recently introduced to the aquarium. If they do not eat for several days, it is generally not serious; however, if the problem per-sists, it could be related to other dif-ficulties, including disease. On the other hand, if the animal appears otherwise normal, its apparent lack of appetite may simply be related to the type of food offered. In that case, you should try a different type of food.

Other causes for not eating could be aggression by other aquarium fish, or simply that the fish is a shy species that normally does not feed in the open when aggressive fish are eating.

You should also keep in mind that if prepared dry foods are offered, it takes time for fish to become accli-mated to this type of food. This is especially true if the fish have been fed mostly live or frozen foods in the pet shop. It is always best to ask the retailer what types of food were used.

Guidelines for Feeding Marine Invertebrates

Invertebrates eat virtually the same food as marine fish; however, the diversity of marine invertebrates and differing feeding habits require that the food be presented in various ways. Many invertebrates, such as clams, mussels, corals, and feather-duster worms, are filter feeders.

Other invertebrates, such as shrimp, lobsters, and hermit crabs, are predatory and carnivorous. Still others, such as certain snails, sea urchins, and nudibranchs, are herbivorous.

Filter-Feeding Invertebrates

Filter-feeding invertebrates must receive ample amounts of food suspended in the water. Clams, for example, will constantly filter large volumes of water to ingest suspended food particles. These particles are passed into the digestive tract from specialized collecting areas with mucus.

Other invertebrates such as corals and small colonial anemones collect small suspended particles and other organisms from the water using their tentacles. Feather-duster worms use their feathery feeding tentacles to catch suspended particles.

Feeding these invertebrates involves supplying suspended food particles that may be live or frozen. A preferred method has been to add newly hatched baby brine shrimp to the aquarium, cease filtration, and allow the invertebrates to feed for 30 to 60 minutes. Then resume filtration.

Various types of commercial frozen invertebrate foods are available that can also be used to feed invertebrates. You must take care in using these foods as they can rapidly foul the aquarium.

Carnivorous Invertebrates

Hermit crabs, lobsters, and shrimp are among the easiest invertebrates to feed. They are active in the aquarium, searching for pieces of food left over after regular fish feedings. Hermit crabs are particularly good in scavenging the aquarium bottom for bits of food.

Sea anemones are popular invertebrates for marine aquariums. There are numerous species, including the well-known large variety, and also smaller colonial species.

Provided with the proper environmental conditions and fed properly, these sea anemones will flourish in almost any aquarium. Sea anemones are best fed by hand. Feeding the sea anemone once a week is usually sufficient to maintain it in a healthy condition.

A piece of fish or shrimp should be placed directly on the anemone's tentacles near the central mouth. The anemone will envelop the food and ingest it.

Herbivorous Invertebrates

Various snails, sea urchins, and some species of nudibranch are herbivorous. Such animals must receive ample supplies of plant material for survival.

In aquariums with growths of algae, small snails and sea urchins will generally do well. Herbivorous nudibranchs will survive fairly well, but carnivorous nudibranchs do poorly in aquariums because of their strict feeding requirements. If an ample amount of algae is not available, you can substitute various types of greens such as lettuce, spinach, or other suitable leaves. Your local pet store may have some advice on this subject.

Feeding Aquatic Animals While You Are Away

Leaving the aquarium animals unfed for several days or a weekend will not threaten their health. With a good supply of algae growth in the aquarium, fish and invertebrates will be nourished by browsing.

If you will be away for several weeks, however, you will have to arrange to have someone feed your fish. To avoid overfeeding, leave explicit instructions on how much to feed daily. It is recommended that specific daily amounts of frozen, freeze-dried, and dry food be weighed out in advance. This prevents accidental overfeeding by an inexperienced caretaker.

Chapter Ten

Diseases of Marine Fish

Marine aquarium fish are susceptible to infectious and noninfectious diseases. Infectious diseases are caused by biological agents such as bacteria or protozoans that attack susceptible fish, reproduce, and are then transmitted to other fish. Noninfectious diseases are nontransmissible and can be caused by a variety of factors, such as poor nutrition or poor water quality.

Many diseases that are unknown in fish in the natural habitat can occur in aquariums under circumstances that favor the disease development. The immune system of healthy aquatic animals protects them from invasion by disease agents. A minor infection can progress to clinical disease only when the balance between the disease agent and the fish or invertebrate shifts in favor of the disease agent.

The outbreak of disease in an aquarium is serious, especially for the new hobbyist who is generally inexperienced in recognition and control of fish diseases. The best approach to control is always prevention—by providing proper environmental conditions, a good program of aquarium maintenance, a sound diet, and by the use of other preventive measures.

To prevent disease outbreaks, it is important to understand how diseases occur. Disease is a process initiated by reduced resistance of the fish. It is a disruption of the delicate balance involving the fish, the environmental conditions, and the disease agents. Research to date strongly shows that the disease process can be initiated by exposure to unfavorable environmental changes such as temperature fluctuations, persistent ammonia concentrations, low oxygen levels, overcrowding, and inadequate diets. Each of these factors can play a role in the initiation and development of a disease. The conditions listed above are referred to as stress factors. These stress factors singly or in combination cause the stress response, which, depending on the intensity and duration, can be either beneficial or potentially hazardous to the fish.

The Stress Response

Environmental stress decreases the natural resistance of a fish, making it susceptible to disease. Stress is often thought of as negative, but the stress response is a beneficial adaptation to unfavorable conditions.

Initially, when a fish is exposed to a stress factor (stressor), the biochemistry of the fish is altered with the release of various hormones. These chemicals have profound effects, preparing the fish for an emergency situation. The detailed biochemical changes accompanying the stress response are complicated and will not be discussed here in detail; however, the result of these changes enables the fish to cope with potentially dangerous circumstances. For example, if a fish is subjected to stress caused by capture or transport, it will respond to the stress response with the release of various chemicals. These chemicals cause a dilation of gill capillaries, increased blood flow to various parts of the body, and the immediate availability of energy nutrients. Once the fish begins to acclimate to the new aquarium conditions, the fish's body chemistry will slowly return to normal. The physiological changes that occur during such stress episodes help the fish to survive a potentially dangerous situation. However, prolonged exposure to such stressors as chronic levels of ammonia in the water will have serious consequences, including interference in the ability to fight infection.

Minimizing stressful situations in aquariums is well within the reach of marine hobbyists through careful management of the environment, performing recommended water maintenance, avoiding overcrowding, and providing a superior diet. However, if disease does occur, you will need to be able to recognize the problem and take immediate action.

Disease Recognition and Prevention

It was pointed out earlier (see page 48) that fish should be carefully selected prior to purchase to be sure they are in good condition. Evaluating a fish's condition is based on careful observations of the fish's behavior and familiarity with common disease agents. Learning how to interpret abnormal behaviors associated with fish disease requires years of experience, but every marine aquarist, with some study and practice, should be able to recognize many of the disease signs.

Disease Recognition

Sick fish alter their normal behavioral patterns in response to a disease agent or environmental changes. Often the sign observed is not specific, but indicative of either infectious disease or noninfectious water-quality or nutrition-related problems. Some disease signs, such as the presence of a parasite on the fish's body, are specific and easily recognized as a sign of infectious disease. For the inexperienced aquarist, caution must be observed in attempting to diagnose a disease problem.

Diseased fish are recognized by various signs, including:
- increased respiration rate
- scratching on objects or the aquarium bottom
- pale coloration
- refusal to eat
- frayed fins
- appearance of body ulcers
- cloudy eyes, and other signs.

These signs do not necessarily indicate the specific cause, only that a health problem is developing. Pale color, for example, could be caused either by improper nutrition, the early stages of an infectious disease, or poor water quality. Increased respiration is a sign easily recognized, and can be in response to an environmental problem such as a low-dissolved oxygen level or to parasites on the gills. Making a diagnosis from one sign is often very difficult. An accurate diagnosis necessitates the gathering of various pieces of information, including water-quality parameters, maintenance data, and close observation of the affected fish's behavior.

The following nonspecific disease signs are commonly associated with marine fish affected with a disease.

Increased Respiration: Fish have an abnormally high rate of breathing, with a tendency to stay near the water surface or areas of high water agitation.

Possible Causes: Water-quality problem such as low oxygen concentrations, high ammonia, or high temperature are likely the cause of increased respiration; the fish could also be infested with external parasites.

Scratching: Marine fish scratch or rub themselves repeatedly on objects in the aquarium or on aquarium bottom.

Possible Causes: Continual scratching is most often associated with parasitic infestation.

Clamped Fins: The affected fish will tend to hold its fins close to the body proper. Frayed fins can sometimes be observed.

Possible Causes: Most fish erect their fins during swimming, though this behavior varies. Fish that tightly clamp their fins and appear to be listless could be in the early stages of disease. If frayed fins are also present, it could indicate that the fish has been in a fight with another fish in the aquarium.

Lethargy: There is a decrease or lack of normal swimming or feeding activity.

Possible Causes: This can be related to infectious disease or too low water temperature. It should not be confused with normal inactivity during sleep periods.

Lack of Appetite: This sign is common and can be caused by various factors. Affected fish refuse to feed or abruptly stop feeding.

Possible Causes: Refusal to eat can be related to feeding an improper type of food, such as feeding dry food to fish that accept only live foods. When fish suddenly stop feeding, it could indicate the early stages of an infectious disease. When this occurs after the introduction of a new aquarium fish, it can be related to the fright response or to aggression by tankmates.

Pale Color: Fish lose their natural coloration and become pale.

Possible Causes: A short-term change in color is normal and can be related to a fright response. This can occur when fish are moved from one tank to another. Chronic pale color can be related to development of disease or poor nutrition. Chronic abnormal light color can also indicate blindness.

Cloudy Eyes: With this easily recognizable sign, either one eye or both eyes become cloudy.

Possible Causes: Physical injury related to capture or netting is not uncommon with new fish. The development of a cloudy eye can also indicate physical injury caused by fighting. The condition is sometimes temporary, while extensive physical damage can result in permanent injury. Cloudy eyes can also be a sign of bacterial or parasitic disease.

Frayed Fins: The fins are either frayed or shredded. The base of the fins may have a reddish appearance.

Possible Causes: This can be caused by injury from fighting with tankmates, or can indicate the early stages of a bacterial or other infectious disease.

White Spots on Body: Affected fish have irregular distribution of white spots over the body.

Possible Causes: This can be caused by external protozoan parasites or by adherence of fine particulate matter or air bubbles in the mucus.

Heavy Secretion of Body Mucus: Fish have an abnormally high increase in the amount of body slime, sometimes with long mucus strings falling off the body.

Possible Causes: This can be caused by poor water quality, such as increased ammonia, high copper, or high pH. The sign may also indicate infestation by protozoan parasites.

Protrusion of Eyes (Exophthalmia): Either one eye or both eyes appear to bulge out of their orbits.

Possible Causes: Eye protrusion can be a sign of an internal problem caused by infectious disease agents such as bacteria, viruses, or parasites. The condition can also be related to noninfectious agents such as tumors.

Ulceration of Body: Small-to-large ulcers on the body may have pale areas and reddened perimeter.

Possible Causes: Ulcers may indicate bacterial infection and/or parasitic infestation.

Swollen Abdomen: The fish appears to be swollen or bloated.

Possible Causes: A swollen abdomen can be an indication of an internal bacterial infection, parasitic infestation, or a tumor. It can also be caused by overeating in certain species of fish.

Diagnosing Diseases and Their Causes

It should now be evident that various disease signs can be caused by agents ranging from environmental abnormalities to biological causes such as parasites. Determining the exact cause is not always possible, but it is important to distinguish between diseases initiated by environmental problems and those caused by disease agents.

Assume, for example, that you have an aquarium with several species of fish. You notice that one fish has an increased respiratory rate. From the disease signs previously discussed, this could be related to an environmental problem such as low oxygen concentration or to parasites. How do you determine the exact cause of the increased breathing rate of the fish?

It is important not to assume immediately that the fish is infested by parasites until you are firmly convinced that the rapid respiration is unrelated to water quality. This is due to the fact that a great majority of problems, especially in new aquariums, are related to water quality. The recommended approach is to first perform a series of water tests, including pH, ammonia, nitrite, and others. Check to make sure all filters and air stones are functioning properly. Ask yourself a series of questions:

• When did I make the last water change?

• Are the results of the water tests within acceptable ranges?

• Did I add any new items such as coral or rock, which could be toxic or contribute to water pollution?

• Have any insecticides, paints, or soaps been near the aquarium?

If everything related to equipment function and the environment appears to be normal, then it is likely that the problem is related to an infectious disease agent. The example presented is a simplistic one, but should give you an idea of how to use a problem-solving approach.

Disease Prevention

It is a basic premise that preventing diseases is the best means of control. Good aquarium-care techniques, regular maintenance, proper nutrition, preventing overcrowding of fish, and use of quarantine aquariums will all minimize the development of disease. A quarantine aquarium is one of the most important methods of preventing the introduction of diseases to your aquarium.

Quarantining Aquarium Fish

Isolating new fish in a separate aquarium is a highly effective means of preventing the introduction of diseases to an established aquarium. Quarantine aquariums are often referred to as "hospital aquariums" or "isolation tanks." The process of quarantine requires a separate small aquarium that will be used exclusively for the isolation of new aquarium fish and invertebrates.

While a quarantine aquarium is not required during the first introduction of fish to your display aquarium, quarantine is recommended for future additions of fish to your main aquarium. The use of quarantine aquariums is based on the assumption that all new marine fish carry some type of disease agent, especially external parasites. During capture, holding, and transport, marine fish are stressed, which in turn decreases their resistance to disease. Parasites are known to multiply rapidly during transport. If diseased fish are added directly to an established display aquarium, they will transmit the disease agents to other fish.

Another benefit of quarantine is that it allows new fish to acclimate to their new conditions in a less stressful environment. New fish directly added to an aquarium are often bullied by the established fish, making it more difficult for the new fish to acclimate.

Setting Up the Quarantine Aquarium

The quarantine aquarium or hospital tank is to be used for the isolation of new fish or invertebrates. The aquarium need not be too large; usually a 10- to 15-gallon (37.8- to 56.7-L) aquarium is sufficient. The size is partially determined by the size of your main aquarium.

The aquarium should be equipped with a filtration system, air stone, heater, and other standard equipment required to maintain good water quality. The aquarium bottom should be covered with a relatively thin layer of substrate if you are using only an outside filter. A few added pieces of coral rock or coral will provide some refuge for new fish.

The parameters of water condition in the quarantine aquarium, including pH, temperature, and salinity, should approximate that of your display aquarium. This will allow a safer transference of the fish to the main aquarium upon completion of the isolation period.

Quarantine Period

The recommended quarantine period for new fish is a minimum of three weeks. The first week is critical, requiring frequent observation of the behavior of your new fish. It is during the first week that you can determine if the new fish are adjusting to their new environment. Mortalities cannot always be avoided, since some fish species are not always capable of the needed adjustment. Any fish found dead in the quarantine aquarium must be removed promptly to prevent increased levels of bacteria and water pollution.

It is recommended that new fish be fed as soon as they begin to show an interest in eating. Hardy species, such as damselfish, are usually the first to respond to the addition of food. Other species, such as butterflyfish, tend to be more sensitive and may not eat for a few days. However, as long as the fish were known to have been eating in the retailer's aquarium prior to purchase, you need not be overly concerned with the initial lack of interest in food. During quarantine, be cautious not to overfeed the new fish, but provide enough for them to obtain adequate nourishment.

All new fish, without exception, must be placed in the quarantine aquarium. Even fish that appear to be in perfect condition could be harboring parasites. This applies also to fish that may have been previously quarantined at a retail store. While retailers will not purposely sell a diseased fish, they are not always able to quarantine the fish long enough prior to sale.

Once the fish are placed into quarantine, additional fish should not be added until the initial group has completed quarantine and has been moved to the display aquarium. In addition, never mix invertebrates and fish together for quarantine. Invertebrates must be treated differently from marine fish.

Although invertebrates such as sea anemones, sea urchins, starfish, coral, and other common aquarium invertebrates do not become actively infected by diseases of fish, they can act as passive carriers. Passive carriers can transmit a parasite that has accidentally become attached to the animals. Therefore, although not absolutely required, quarantining of invertebrates adds another dimension of disease control by further minimizing disease agent transmission.

Upon completion of the quarantine period, if the fish or invertebrates appear healthy, they can be transferred to your main aquarium. If not, they should remain in quarantine for an additional few weeks or more.

Quarantine Treatment Methods

New fish need to be treated with chemical preparations to eradicate possible external parasites and to control any possible secondary bacterial infections. Various medications are available for treating the most common marine fish diseases. You should rely on your retailer for selecting the appropriate medication for treatment of marine fish during quarantine.

It should be pointed out that while various medications are commonly used during quarantine for treatment of fish, they should never be used for treating invertebrates. The majority of invertebrates are extremely sensitive to chemicals, at substantially lower concentrations than those used to treat fish. Invertebrates, therefore, should be left in the quarantine aquarium for three weeks without the addition of any medication.

Although a more detailed description of the appropriate chemicals will be discussed later in this chapter, some introductory remarks are in order.

Copper. Various chemicals are available for use during quarantine to control parasitic infestations and bacterial infections. Some of the products most widely used to control common external parasites contain copper. These medications have been used for over three decades as the most reliable means of eradicating serious protozoan parasites of marine fish. Specifically, they have been used to control white spot disease and coral reef disease (see discussion of these diseases later in this chapter).

Copper-based medications are widely available under various trade names. Make sure that the active ingredient, noted on the label, is copper sulfate, copper sulfate pentahydrate, or other copper compounds. Such solutions also contain additional ingredients such as citric acid. These solutions are commonly referred to as "free copper" or "ionic copper." These differ from other copper-based solutions that are known as "chelated copper." Chelated copper-based products differ chemically from ionic copper. Do not purchase chelated copper medications, as these are not as effective in eradicating parasites and can cause serious problems for your aquarium and fish. If you are unsure of the type of copper solution to purchase, you should rely on the advice of your pet shop retailer.

Copper can be very toxic to fish when not used properly, and no treatment should begin unless a copper test kit is available for monitoring the copper concentration in the water. Since copper is removed through the interaction with various chemicals in seawater, additional booster doses must be added periodically to maintain the proper concentration. Although the procedure can differ according to the copper medication used, the following is the generalized procedure for treatment with copper.

Add the proper amount of copper solution to the aquarium water according to the label instructions to produce a concentration of 0.12 to 0.18 mg/L (ppm). Perform a copper test every day to ensure that the concentration is within the acceptable range. The initial concentration should be brought up to 0.18 mg/L. It is important that the concentration not exceed the upper range or decrease below the lower limit. The treatment must continue uninterrupted for a minimum of 21 days. Upon completion of the treatment, a partial water change should be made to assist in reducing any residual copper in the water. Since copper is toxic to invertebrates, they must never be added to the quarantine tank just after a copper treatment.

Organophosphates: In addition to copper, there are other chemicals available for controlling marine parasites; copper alone is not able to

▶*Top left: The Flame Scallop (Lima lima) does well in aquariums if supplied with adequate supplies of brine shrimp and other foods. Top right: The Cowrie (Cypraea spadicea). Center left: The Nudibranch (Chromodoris bullocki). Center right: The Nudibranch (Chromodoris spp.). Bottom left: The Nudibranch (Hypselodoris spp.). Bottom right: The Octopus (Octopus hummelincki).*

control every type of parasite affecting marine fish. Organophosphates or formalin-based products are recommended for eradication of worm-like parasites called flukes (see discussion, page 148), commonly present on various species of marine fish. The treatments can be concurrent with the copper treatment. You should rely on your local retailer to obtain either of these medications together with instructions for their correct use.

Antibiotics: Although external parasites are the major disease-causing agents of new marine fish, it is sometimes necessary to use antibiotics to control bacterial infections. Injuries sustained during netting, frayed fins due to aggressive behavior with other fish, or severe external parasitic infestation can often require treatment to prevent a serious infection. Antibiotics must be used carefully to prevent overuse in treating every suspected bacterial infection.

Common Diseases of Marine Fish

The common diseases of marine fish have been grouped into four areas. Only the most commonly occurring problems will be covered here; a more detailed presentation is beyond the scope of this book.

Health problems of marine fish can be caused by parasites, microbes, deterioration in water quality, or poor nutrition practices.

Parasites: By far, parasites are the most common and troublesome disease agents of marine fishes. Various parasites can be found on marine fish, including protozoa, worms, or crustacea. They affect the fish by attachment to the skin, gills, or sometimes the eye. Other parasites are internal, where they invade the muscles, liver, or other organs. While some parasites are easily visible, others cannot be seen without a microscope.

Microbes: Microbial diseases are caused by bacteria, fungi, and viruses. Microbes are so small they cannot be seen with the naked eye. They are responsible for a variety of diseases affecting marine aquarium fish. The most serious microbial diseases are caused by bacteria, which readily infect stressed fish.

Water Quality: Diseases can be initiated by poor water quality conditions, including high ammonia concentrations, low oxygen, improper pH, the presence of chloramines, or dangerous levels of other toxic chemicals. Diseases related to altered environmental conditions are not infectious, but chronic exposure to poor water quality can cause either immediate death or a secondary infection by bacteria.

Nutrition: Diseases caused by poor nutrition are not uncommon in aquarium fish. Various deficiency syndromes include stunted growth, blindness, starvation, poor color, or excessive fat deposition. Nutritional problems are more readily apparent in rapidly growing young fish.

Parasitic Diseases

Parasitic diseases are a major problem for aquarium fishes. Almost all marine fish have parasites to a some degree. Protozoans, small microscopic animals generally invisible to the naked eye, are the most serious types of parasites. There are numerous parasites responsible for diseases of marine fish; this discussion will be limited to the most common parasitic problems known to occur under aquarium conditions: coral reef disease *(Amyloodinium)*, white spot disease *(Cryptocaryon)*, clownfish disease *(Brooklynella)*, black ich (worm parasites), flukes (gill and body worm parasites), copepods (crustacean parasites).

Coral Reef Disease *(Amyloodinium ocellatum):* This is one of the most common diseases of marine fish; it can rapidly cause death if not treated promptly. The parasite, a small protozoan, primarily attacks the gills, body, and fins of the fish. It is introduced into the aquarium through nonquarantined fish.

The parasites appear as fine, dustlike, white to yellowish spots, most readily visible to the naked eye on the transparent portions of the fins or dark pigmented areas of the body. Other signs associated with the disease include scratching on the aquarium bottom and on rocks, increased respiration rate, gasping near the water surface, pale color, and appearance of excessive slime on the fish's body.

The disease is rapidly transmitted from infested fish to other fish in the aquarium. During the life cycle of the parasite, it first develops on the fish's body (the host) and, when mature, drops to the aquarium bottom. The parasite encysts, then undergoes cell multiplication to form small free-swimming parasites called dinospores. These young parasites are released from the cyst and infect other marine fish.

Treatment: Coral reef disease must be treated as soon as the disease is identified. A delay in treatment can result in the death of all your aquarium fish. The treatment of choice is through the use of ionic copper medications. As discussed in the quarantine section (see page 139), you should purchase only ionic

Some common diseases of marine fish include lymphocystis, a viral disease (top); fin rot, often caused by bacteria (center); and black ich, caused by a small worm (bottom).

copper medications, not chelated copper.

Regardless of the brand of copper medicine you use, it is essential that the treatment be not less than 14 days. The copper must be maintained within the range of 0.12 to 0.18 mg/L. Do not exceed the recommended concentration, as this could cause damage to your fish. Treatments using copper-based medications must never be conducted without the use of a copper test kit to monitor the concentration of copper during the treatment period.

Copper treatments can safely be done in the display aquarium, but keep in mind that copper is toxic to various marine invertebrates. If invertebrates are present, they must be removed prior to the treatment procedure. They should not be returned to the aquarium until the concentration of copper drops below 0.03 mg/L.

White Spot Disease (Crypto-caryon irritans): Also known as saltwater ich, this disease affects the gills, fins, and body of the fish. The parasite is introduced to the aquarium through the addition of infested fish.

Fish infected with the disease develop randomly distributed white spots over the body and fins. The white spots are considerably larger than the small dustlike spots of coral reef disease. Diseased fish tend to scratch on aquarium objects, have a rapid breathing rate, congregate near areas of high water agitation, and stop eating.

White spot disease is caused by a small ciliated protozoan that has a life cycle similar to that of the protozoan that causes coral reef disease. After the attached parasite matures, it drops to the bottom of the aquarium and encysts. While encysted, free-swimming parasites develop and are released into the aquarium water. The free-swimming parasites are then able to infect aquarium fish.

Treatment: White spot disease is treated with copper-based medications as outlined for the treatment of coral reef disease. The copper concentration must be maintained within a range of 0.12 to 0.18 mg/L. However, for complete eradication, the treatment must be maintained for not fewer than 21 days, rather than the 14 days recommended for the treatment of coral reef disease. White spot tends to be more difficult to eradicate, hence the necessity for an extended treatment period.

Clownfish Disease (Brook-lynella hostilis): This is a serious malady affecting clownfish (*Amphib-rion* spp.) or sea horses, and other kinds of marine fish. Various species of clownfish are particularly susceptible to infection from this parasite.

The disease is caused by a small ciliated protozoan invisible to the naked eye. It is a parasite of the gills and skin, and unlike the other protozoans discussed, the life cycle is simple, with the parasite reproducing by cell division. As a result, the parasite multiplies rapidly on affected fish, causing mortalities in a short period of time.

Affected fish develop body lesions, excessive slime secretion, and increased respiration. In the early stages of the disease, all you will notice is an abnormal paleness of color and a rapid breathing rate. As the disease worsens, you will observe lesions on the body, with sloughing of the skin, as well as mucus. The development of a secondary infection with bacteria often accompanies infestation with the parasite.

Treatment: Clownfish disease is capable of killing fish within 24 to 36 hours after the appearance of the signs of scratching and heavy respiration. Prompt treatment must be instituted if the disease is suspected. The parasite is sensitive to various medications, which can be purchased under various trade names. It is recommended that fish with clownfish disease be treated with medications that contain formalin or malachite green. Medications containing copper should be avoided, as the disease is not readily controlled by copper-based chemicals.

Black Ich (turbellarian worms): Known from various species of marine fish from Hawaii and the Indo-Pacific region, the disease was first noted in surgeonfish such as the Yellow Tang *(Zebrasoma flavescens)* and the Sailfin Tang *(Zebrasoma veliferum)*. However, it is also known to afflict various other species, including angelfish and wrasses.

Black ich disease appears as small black spots distributed over the fish's body. The spots are about half the size of a pinhead or smaller. They are primarily found on the body and are especially easy to see on light-colored body areas or on the transparent portions of the fins. Affected fish will scratch on the aquarium bottom or on other objects. Other signs of the disease include lethargy, development of a pale body color, and lack of appetite.

The disease is caused by a small worm known as a turbellarian. After parasitizing a fish, the worms develop on the fish's skin and gills and acquire a dark pigmentation. They are freely mobile and will tend to move over the surface of the fish. After five or six days, depending on the environmental conditions, they drop off the fish to the aquarium bottom. There they mature, with the development of the young worms within their body. Once development of the young is complete, the adult worm bursts, releasing the free-swimming young that infest new host fish.

Treatment: The worms can be controlled with various commercially available medications. Formalin-based products or those containing organophosphate compounds such as trichlorfon appear to be the best medications. In addition to the use of medications, any excessive buildup of organic material and debris should be siphoned from the aquarium several times during treatment. Since the young worms develop on the aquarium bottom, the removal of debris will aid in controlling the disease by reducing their numbers.

Flukes (gill and body worms):
Flukes, or monogenetic (requiring one host) trematodes, are external parasites that attach to the skin and gills of marine fish. Flukes are classified into numerous species, with some easily seen on affected fish and others too small to be seen with the naked eye. As with other parasites, flukes are introduced into the aquarium by nonquarantined fish.

Flukes attach to fish by means of a special organ called a haptor, which is equipped with hooks, clamps, and anchors used to firmly attach the worm to the fish. Flukes are freely motile, moving over the surface of the skin or gills, causing extensive damage to the fish through their movements.

Flukes reproduce on the fish, with sonic species producing hundreds of eggs on the gills and body, which then hatch into free-swimming larvae. The larvae reinfect the host fish or attach to other fish. Other fluke species are viviparous, meaning they give birth to living young instead of producing eggs.

Affected fish show various abnormal behavior changes, including scratching, which is the most obvious sign of infestation. Other signs include increased respiration and change in body color. In severe infestations ulcerations may also be noticeable.

Treatment: These troublesome parasites can be controlled by various treatments, including freshwater dips, formalin-based medications, or the use of organophosphates. Freshwater dips are easily performed and often are very effective in reducing the number of flukes on the body of the fish. The dips are conducted by placing a marine fish briefly into a container of conditioned fresh water with the same pH and temperature as the marine aquarium water. The fish is left in the dip for three to eight minutes, depending on the species of fish. The fish must be carefully watched until it begins to turn on its side. At this point the fish must be promptly returned to the aquarium. The procedure must be done carefully, as not all fish can tolerate this type of treatment; when done properly, however, it will eradicate large numbers of flukes. If you have never conducted a freshwater dip treatment, it is important to discuss it with your local fish retailer before attempting the treatment.

Formalin-based medications and organophosphates have been used for many years with excellent success in treating flukes. Various commercial medications are available specifically for treating flukes on marine fishes.

Copepods (crustacean parasites): These are one of several groups of crustacean parasites affecting the gills and body of marine fishes. Because of their size, copepods are generally easily recognizable on fish. Various species of copepods are species-specific, meaning they will parasitize only one species of fish. If other species of fish are present in the aquarium, they will not become infested.

The obvious sign of infestation is an attached wormlike organism that can be seen on a portion of the fish's body. Only the females of copepods attach to fish, so the worm is readily recognized by the presence of egg strings. Since many species of copepods embed themselves deeply into the host by means of specialized mouthparts, a raised inflamed ring can be seen at the sight of attachment. Copepods are capable of causing severe damage to the host fish, especially when they attach to the gills.

A typical, simplified life cycle of a copepod involves the development of the adult female parasite on the host, with development of egg strings. These egg strings vary in appearance and can be straight, serpentine, or coiled. Upon maturation, the free-swimming larvae hatch from the eggs to seek another fish as a host. The larvae develop into adults and mate. The male then dies while the female attaches to the host to continue the life cycle.

Treatment: It is often difficult to control all species of copepods. Those that are embedded deeply in the fish are impossible to remove without killing the fish in the process. Other species of copepods can be controlled through the use of various medications, including formalin and organophosphates. Organophosphates such as trichlorfon are recommended for treatment. These medications are highly effective in killing the young copepods once they are released from the eggs. A series of treatments over several weeks must be conducted for complete eradication. Various commercial medications are available for controlling copepods in marine aquariums.

Fungal, Bacterial, and Viral Diseases

Funguses, bacteria, and viruses are responsible for various diseases of marine aquarium fish. Collectively, this group of disease agents are referred to as microbes. All are so small that it is not possible to see the organism without the use of a microscope. Identification of diseases caused by these organisms must initially rely on external signs such as skin lesions or nodules.

Microbial disease outbreaks in aquariums are correlated with a deterioration of water quality, parasites that damage the fish's skin or gills, or poor nutrition. Any trauma that weakens the fish's disease resistance barriers allows invasion by microbes. Microbial diseases are readily transmitted from one fish to another.

Fungal Infections: Fungal infections of marine fish are known from various species including sea horses, butterflyfish, and clownfish; however, fungal infections are relatively uncommon in marine fish. Infection often follows prior damage to a fish, caused by handling with a net or by an existing infection by parasites.

Aquarium hobbyists familiar with fungal infections of freshwater fishes will be familiar with the characteristic white, cottonlike growth of fungus on the skin or fins of infected fish. Known as *Saprolegnia* sp., this fungus readily invades stressed freshwater fish, but is not known to affect marine fishes. Signs of fungal infection in marine fish are therefore less dramatic and often difficult to distinguish.

When present, the fungus appears on marine fishes as a fine film, dark pigmented areas, or a coating covering areas of the body or gills. This coating can easily be confused with similar signs that are caused by the presence of various types of parasites.

Treatment: Treatment of fungal infections of the body and gills involves the use of various fungicides available commercially. Malachite green and methylene blue have been used successfully to control fungal infections in marine fish. Various drugs are also useful for controlling both fungal and bacterial infections. Since fungus is a secondary invader, treatment methods must also address the initial cause of the disease, including trauma induced by deteriorated water quality, poor nutrition, or poor handling of the fish.

Bacterial Infections: These are also commonly associated with pre-existing trauma or stress of marine fish, including poor water quality, handling trauma, and poor nutrition. Pathogenic bacteria—those that can cause disease—as well as the beneficial nitrifying bacteria are always present in aquarium water. The pathogenic bacteria will initiate disease only if the fish's immune system is impaired. Providing optimal water quality, controlling the presence of parasites, and practicing good aquarium management will prevent the outbreak of bacterial diseases. The exact identification of bacteria requires the use of sophisticated diagnostic tests routinely used by laboratory technicians. The procedures involve growing the bacteria on specialized media, then conducting various chemical tests.

Many bacterial infections can be identified by various signs they produce when they infect fish. Bacterial infections can be divided into those causing external infections and those primarily causing internal lesions. It must be noted that external infections can rapidly worsen, spreading to the internal organs and bloodstream. Bacteria can enter fish either through the skin or by oral ingestion.

External bacterial infections (fin-and-tail rot and ulcer disease) can be caused by various species of bacteria. Bacteria most commonly associated with these infections include *pseudomonas, myxobacteria,* and *vibrio.* The latter group is the major cause of bacterial infections, especially in newly imported fish that are still under extreme stress from capture and transport.

Collectively, the signs of external infections caused by these bacteria are often referred to as "fin-and-tail rot" and "ulcer" disease. The names refer to the signs of infections from bacterial disease and not to their cause from specific bacteria.

Signs associated with bacterial infections of the body, fins, or gills include deterioration of the fins, fraying, and inflammation. When the infection involves the fins, portions of the fins will begin to disintegrate, exposing the fin rays. Ulceration of the body is also associated with bacterial infections, with the appearance of large, reddened, inflamed lesions that expand rapidly to involve larger portions of the body. Affected fish will become listless, will tend to hide, and in advanced stages will cease feeding.

Treatment: Bacterial infections must be treated promptly because of the rapid progression of the disease from minor to severe. Various antimicrobials are available for treating bacterial diseases of marine fish. Those recommended for the treatment of external infections of the body surface include nitrofurazone, nifurpirinol, and various sulfonamides. Although various antimicrobials are available commercially for the treatment of bacterial infections, not all are suitable for use in marine aquariums. Those that are virtually useless for treatment of infections in marine aquariums include ampicillin, penicillin, tetracycline, and erythromycin. The latter can kill the nitrifying bacteria in your aquarium, causing an increase in toxic ammonia.

In addition to treating your aquarium, you should also investigate other possible causes of the outbreak, including the addition of non-quarantined fish, excessively high water temperatures, an overcrowded aquarium, low-dissolved oxygen, or other parameters that could have initiated the infection.

Mycobacteriosis (fish tuberculosis) is transmitted from one fish to another through the ingestion of bacteria-contaminated food. It is important to understand that this disease is not infectious to humans.

Mycobacteriosis is a disease of older fish or those maintained in aquarium environments that favor proliferation of the bacteria. High concentrations of organics, the buildup of debris in filter beds, poor filtration, and overcrowding favor the outbreak of this disease.

The signs of the disease differ with the species of fish as well as the extent of infection. Typically, fish can develop a pronounced swelling of the body with a change in normal body coloration. The appearance of signs associated with mycobacteriosis is largely dependent on the stage of the disease. Fish in advanced stages become emaciated, have swollen or cloudy eyes, and can develop ulcers on the body.

Although the general signs are useful in attempting to recognize a possible infection, diagnosis can be confirmed only from microscopic examination of the internal organs of the fish. Mycobacteria characteristically infect various internal organs, where they form tubercules. If a fish is in the later stages of the disease or is suspected of having died from mycobacteriosis, you may wish to have a veterinarian do a necropsy.

Treatment: Mycobacteriosis is untreatable. Prevention is the only protection. Although various medications are sold with claims to cure the disease, no scientific data back these claims. Fish suspected of harboring the disease, or that seem to have died from it, should be removed promptly from the aquarium to prevent transmission.

Viruses: Marine fish are also susceptible to infection by viruses, although few have been identified from aquarium fish. Viruses are smaller than bacteria and require the use of sophisticated electron microscopes for their identification.

The major virus common among marine fishes and relatively easy to identify from the lesions it produces is lymphocystis. The disease is chronic, meaning that in the majority of cases it will not kill the infected fish. The major consequence of lymphocystis disease is disfigurement of the fish.

The disease agent preferentially infects the cells of the skin and fins, causing the appearance of lesions. Once the virus infects a cell, it takes over the activities of the cell, forcing it to manufacture more viruses.

Lymphocystis is recognized by the appearance of large nodular lesions that form white-to-cream clusters. The clusters are hard to the touch because of the formation of an outer layer of cartilage. The lesions most often appear on the trailing portions of the fins, on the body proper, or on the lips of the fish. The normal behavior of the fish is rarely affected, with the exception of infection of the mouth. Infection of the mouth and development of the lesions can interfere with normal feeding behavior.

Lymphocystis is spread when infected fish die, decay, and release viral particles. Research on the disease has shown that the virus easily infects fish that have injured skin from rough handling or fighting with other fish.

Treatment: There is no known cure for lymphocystis. The use of medications including antibiotics appears to be useless. If the lesions are restricted to the distal area of a fin, it is possible to carefully trim off the infected portion and treat with an antibiotic to prevent a bacterial infection. In many cases, however, the virus will reappear in the same area.

Water-Quality-Induced Diseases

As previously pointed out, maintaining proper water quality is critical for ensuring the health and vitality of marine fish. Various disorders can be related to water quality problems. Such problems, briefly touched

◄ Top left: Starfish, such as this brilliant red starfish (Fromia sp.), are generally easy to maintain in aquariums. Top right: Brittlestars are not the best invertebrates for aquariums because they tend to hide under rocks. Bottom left: Sea urchins need the proper amount of algae in order to thrive in an aquarium. Bottom right: The Sea Apple (Psudocolochirus violaceus) makes a unique aquarium invertebrate.

upon in early chapters, will now be discussed in more detail.

While infectious diseases generally follow a pattern of staggered deaths over several days or weeks, a deterioration in water quality will affect the entire aquarium population, resulting in rapid fish mortalities. Water quality problems are still the major cause of death of marine fish in aquariums, even more serious than the infectious diseases discussed in the beginning of this chapter. As pointed out, the stress induced by poor water quality opens the way for infection by bacteria and other disease agents.

Various categories of common toxic conditions will be discussed below in relation to water quality deterioration in the aquarium.

Nitrogen Compounds: Ammonia, nitrite, and nitrate formed during the process of nitrification can all have serious consequences for the health of fish and invertebrates. Ammonia and nitrite pose more of a problem than nitrate, the least toxic of these compounds.

Ammonia is the most toxic to marine organisms. As ammonia accumulates in the bloodstream and in the tissues, affected organisms are unable to transport oxygen properly. Sensitive marine animals succumb rapidly to very low concentrations of ammonia. As we pointed out in an earlier chapter, the higher the pH and temperature, the greater the proportion of toxic ammonia formed.

The accumulation of ammonia is most serious when conditioning is still in process, or when there is excess decaying food in the aquarium, overcrowding of fish, and/or inadequate filtration. Chronic ammonia concentrations will predispose fish to other diseases and will kill those species that are most sensitive to high ammonia concentrations.

Fish affected by ammonia poisoning will appear listless, will show an increased respiration rate, and can develop other opportunistic bacterial infections. An ammonia test must be performed if any of these signs are observed in the aquarium. In the event of abnormal concentrations, you should make an immediate water change to reduce the ammonia concentration. If the source is overcrowding, you should move some of the fish to another holding aquarium.

Although nitrite is less toxic than ammonia, fish can still be harmed by the accumulation of this toxin. Sensitive fish such as butterflyfish will not tolerate nitrite.

High concentrations of nitrite are generally a serious problem only during the aquarium conditioning period. High nitrite affects fish by preventing the normal uptake of oxygen. As with ammonia, the concentration of nitrite is reduced by making water changes.

Nitrate is the least toxic of the nitrogen products, although tolerance of nitrate varies among species of fish and invertebrates. However, despite its greatly reduced toxicity, accumulations of nitrate are known to affect the normal growth of fish and the survivability of invertebrates.

Invertebrates will not tolerate chronic high concentrations of nitrate.

Regular water changes will reduce the amount of nitrate. The easiest way to control the buildup of excessive nitrate is to allow some controlled growth of algae in the aquarium. In addition, keeping the filter running efficiently, avoiding crowding of animals in the aquarium, as well as not overfeeding minimize the buildup of nitrate.

Chlorine and Chloramines: All municipal water supplies are treated either with chlorine or chloramines to purify the water for human consumption. Chlorine has been the most widely used for water purification, but in recent years chloramina-

▲ *The Tobacco Basslet* (Serranus tabacarius).

tion has been replacing chlorination. Detoxifying tap water to destroy chlorine has been easily accomplished by simply adding a chlorine remover or multipurpose water conditioners. When these are added, chlorine is destroyed and the water can be used safely for the aquarium. However, the situation is more complicated when municipal water is treated with chloramine.

Both chlorine and chloramine are toxic to fish and invertebrates, but chloramines differ in many respects from chlorine. Chloramines can be thought of as a combination of ammonia and chlorine. Chemically, they are very stable in water. In addition, they pass readily through the gills of fish, compared with chlorine, which does not easily enter the bloodstream. When a water conditioner is added to water containing chloramines, the chloramine is destroyed, but what is left is ammonia, also toxic to fish and invertebrates. In addition, some water companies tend to add an excess of ammonia to the water when producing chloramines, which means that some ammonia may already be present before you use a water conditioner to destroy the chloramine.

Fish affected with chloramine poisoning will show abnormal swimming behavior. They tend to remain motionless or rock in a side-to-side motion. Some fish will also rest on the bottom of the aquarium and cease feeding. Death from chloramine or chlorine toxicity is rapid.

To avoid poisoning by either chlorine or chloramine, always use a water conditioner to prepare the water for use. Whenever you make water changes, you must also treat the water to destroy these toxins. If you suspect chloramines are added to your water, you should call your municipal water company and ask if they are using the chloramination process. If they are, you will need to ensure that all water is treated to destroy the chloramines and to reduce the concentration of ammonia. You can reduce ammonia concentrations by either using activated carbon or specific ammonia-removing chemicals that are available commercially. It is also recommended that you acquire a total chlorine test kit for measuring chlorine and chloramines.

Heavy Metals: Copper, lead, aluminum, and others are very toxic to marine fish. Copper medications are useful for controlling various disease agents when used at specific concentrations; however, in high concentrations, copper is capable of killing fish. Invertebrates cannot be exposed to any copper.

Heavy metals can be introduced to the aquarium by the use of contaminated water, the introduction of decorative items that contain heavy metals, or the addition of chemicals.

Municipal water supplies can also be a source of copper (some municipalities add copper to their reservoirs to control the growth of algae). Copper and other metals can also be introduced when water is passed through metal piping or stored in galvanized buckets. Copper poisoning through overdosage can occur when copper medications are added to the aquarium for treatment, but the water is not properly monitored with a copper test kit.

Fish affected by heavy metal poisoning generally show similar signs of poisoning with other toxins in the water. The fish will become lethargic, develop increased respiration, cease eating, and die rapidly.

In order to prevent metal poisoning of aquarium fish, always use water conditioners that contain special chemicals to render heavy metals nontoxic. In addition, never store water in metal containers, and check with your water company to see if they ever add metal compounds to the water to control algae in reservoirs. If you suspect you live in a building with copper piping, use a copper test kit to check the water prior to using it in an aquarium.

Pesticides: Commonly used for eradicating insects, these are often very toxic to fish and invertebrates. It is important to protect the aquarium from accidental poisoning by these products. If you must use sprays, be sure to cover the aquarium and temporarily disconnect the air pump to prevent the insecticide from being pumped into the water. Depending on the size of the aquarium and number of fish, the filtration and air pumps should not be disconnected for several hours. Before starting again, make sure the room is well ventilated to remove any residual airborne insecticides.

Fish affected with pesticides will demonstrate a variety of signs of toxicity. They will gasp at the water surface, lose their normal color, and swim abnormally. As with other water toxicity, all the fish will be affected. If you suspect that the water has been contaminated with a pesticide, you must make a major water change to reduce the toxin. In addition, change the activated carbon in the filter and continue normal filtration. Activated carbon is capable of rapidly removing many pesticides from water.

Nutrition-Related Diseases

In an earlier chapter on nutrition (see page 119) it was pointed out that deficiencies in nutrients can induce disease. The majority of diet-related problems can easily be averted by providing a variety of foods.

Diseases related to deficiencies, including inadequate protein and vitamins, appear to be the major problem with marine fish. On the other hand, feeding inappropriate food or excessive amounts of food can also be detrimental. Fatty degeneration of the liver occurs when marine fish have too much fat in their diet.

Starvation is one of the most serious problems of aquarium fish. A refusal of fish to feed for more than several days can be related to infectious disease, aggression by tankmates, or disinterest in the type of food offered. Some species of fish are specialized in their feeding requirements; it is not uncommon for them to refuse various foods. Make sure you know what the fish have been eating before you purchase them.

It is not unusual for a fish to refuse to eat for several days after introduction to a new aquarium. This should be considered normal. Generally, within a few days fish will begin eating properly. If the fish continue to refuse to feed, make sure that this is not related to aggression from other tankmates. If this is not the cause, offer some other types of food, including live foods. In the majority of cases, this will solve the problem.

Appendices

Appendix 1: Useful Reference Information

Volume
1 U.S. gallon = 3.785 liters
1 teaspoon = 5 milliliters
1 milliliter = 1 cubic centimeter
1 liter = 1,000 milliliters
1 milligram per liter = 1 part per million
1 ounce = 29.6 milliliters

Weight
1 pound = 0.45 kilograms
1 kilogram = 2.2 pounds
1 ounce = 28.4 grams

Length
1 inch = 2.54 centimeters
1 foot = 0.3 meters
1 meter = 3.28 feet

Appendix 2: Miscellaneous Reference Information

To Convert Fahrenheit Temperatures to Centigrade:
A) Subtract 32 from the Fahrenheit temperature.
B) Divide by 1.8.

Example: What is 75°F in Centigrade?
Solution: 75 − 32 = 43
              43 ÷ 1.8 = 23.9°C

To Convert Centigrade Temperatures to Fahrenheit:
A) Multiply the Centigrade temperature by 1.8.
B) Add 32.

Example: What is 30°C in Fahrenheit?
Solution: 30 × 1.8 = 54
              54 + 32 = 86°F

◄Top: The Flame Hawkfish (Neocirrhitus armatus)
is a well-known and hardy aquarium fish. Bottom:
The Longnosed Hawkfish (Oxycirrhites typus) uses
its long snout to probe crevices for food.

Useful Addresses and Literature

Associations

The Breeder's Registry
P.O. Box 255373
Sacramento, CA 95865

International Marine Aquarist
  Association (IMAA)
27 Arlesey Road
Henlow, Beds SG16 6DF
United Kingdom

Marine Aquarium Society of
  Los Angeles (MASLA)
1016 Burtonwood Avenue
Thousand Oaks, CA 91360

Marine Aquarium Society of
  North America
1426 Hidden River Road
Horse Cave, KY 42749

Books

Goodson, G. *Fishes of the Atlantic Coast.* Palos Verdes, California: Marquest Colorguide Books, 1976.

Gratzek, J. B., editor. *Aquariology: The Science of Fish Health Management.* Morris Plains, New Jersey: Tetra Press, 1992.

Lewbart, G. A. *Self-Assessment Color Review of Ornamental Fish.* Ames, Iowa: Iowa State University Press, 1998.

Sprung, J., J. C. Delbeek. *The Reef Aquarium.* Coconut Grove, Florida: Ricordea Publishing Inc., 1997.

Stadelmann, Peter. *Setting Up an Aquarium.* Hauppauge, New York: Barron's Educational Series, Inc., 2000.

Ward, Brian. *The Aquarium Fish Survival Manual.* Hauppauge, New York: Barron's Educational Series, Inc., 1985.

Magazines

Aquarium Fish
2401 Beverly Blvd.
Los Angeles, CA 90057

Freshwater and Marine Aquarium
144 W. Sierra Madre Blvd.
Sierra Madre, CA 91024

Index

Acanthuridae, 75–76
Acanthurus
  coeruleus, 76
  leucosternon, 76
Acclimation
  invertebrates, 84
  marine fish, 50
Acrylic aquarium, 5
Aggression, 51
Air pump, 19
Air stone/diffuser, 19, 111
Algae:
  lighting requirements, 22–24
  macroalgae species, 41–43
  species, 40–41
Aluteres scriptus, 79
Amino acids, 121
Ammonia, 9–10, 31, 101, 154
Ammonification, 102
Amphiprion
  ocellaris, 61
  sebae, 61
Anemonefishes, 61
Angelfishes, 53–54
Anisotremus virginicus, 65
Annelida, 87–89
Antibiotics, 144
Apogon
  binotatus, 60
  cyanosoma, 60
  maculatus, 60
Apogonidae, 59–60
Appearance, 48
Aquarium. *See* Marine aquarium
Arothron
  hispidus, 69
  reticularis, 69
Arrow Crabs, 90–91
Atlantic Blue Chromis, 62
Atlantic Sea Horse, 74

Bacteria:
  aerobic, 10
  anaerobic, 10, 88
  Nitrobacter, 10, 103, 105
  Nitrosomonas, 9–10, 103–105

Bacterial diseases, 150–151, 153
Balistapus undulatus, 78
Balistes vetula, 78
Balistidae, 77–79
Balistoides conspicillum, 78
Banggai Cardinalfish, 60
Bannerfish, 57
Barhead Rabbitfish, 70
Barred Flamefish, 60
Basslets, 54–55
Batfishes, 55
Bicolor Basslet, 55
Bicolor Blenny, 56
Bicolored Parrotfish, 67–68
Bigeye Soldierfish, 75
Bird Wrasse, 81
Blackcap Basslet, 54
Black ich, 147
Blennies, 55–56
Blenniidae, 55–56
Blue Damsel, 62
Bluehead, 81
Blue-Lined Snapper, 74–75
Blue-Lined Triggerfish, 78
Blue-Spotted Boxfish, 80
Blue-Spotted Jawfish, 66
Blue-Spotted Parrotfish, 68
Blue Tang, 76
Bodianus mesothorax, 81
Body temperature, 120
Bottom materials, 33–35
Boxer Crabs, 91
Boxfish, 79–80
Brine shrimp, 125–127
Brittlestars, 98
Bryopsis, 40
Buffers, 28–29, 115
Butterflyfishes, 56–57, 59

Calcareous materials, 33–35
Callionymidae, 62–63
Carbohydrates, 122
Cardinalfishes, 59–60
Carnivores, 121
Caulerpa, 41
  ashmeadii, 42
  mexicana, 42
  prolifera, 42
  racemosa, 42

Centropyge
  bispinosus, 53–54
  flavissimus, 54
  loriculus, 54
Cephalopholis miniata, 72
Cetoscarus bicolor, 67–68
Chaetodon
  aunga, 59
  lunula, 59
  meyeri, 59
  omatissimus, 59
Chaetodontidae, 56–57, 59
Chelmon rosiratus, 57–58
Chilomycterus schoepfi, 68
Chloramines, 35, 155–156
Chlorine, 35, 155–156
Chromis
  caerulea, 62
  cyanea, 62
Cirrhitidae, 65–66
Cladophora, 40
Clams, 93, 95
  fresh or frozen, 128
Clownfish disease, 146–147
Clownfishes, 61
Clown Sweetlips, 65
Clown Triggerfish, 78
Clown Wrasse, 81
Cnidarians, 85–87
Community aquarium, 50–51, 84–85
Compatibility of species, 51–52
Conditioning period, 26, 35, 101–106
Copepods, 148–149
Copper, 141–142, 146
Copperband, 57–58
Coral:
  artificial, 38–39
  natural, 38
Coral Beauty Angelfish, 53–54
Coral reef disease, 145–146
Corals (live), 85–87
Coris
  aygula, 80
  formosa, 81
  gaimard, 81
Cover, aquarium, 22

Cowfish, 79–80
Crabs, 90–91
Croakers, 63
Cromileptes altivelis, 72
Crustacea, 89–93

Damselfishes, 60–62
Dascyllus
  aruanus, 62
  trimaculatus, 61–62
Dendrochirus
  biocellatus, 72
  zebra, 70, 72
Dentrification, 15, 103
Derbesia, 40
Dietary requirements, 121–123, 125
Diodon hystrix, 68
Diodontidae, 68
Diseases, 135
  microbial, 149–151, 153
  nutrition-related, 157
  parasitic, 145–149
  preventing, 139
  quarantine, 139–142, 144
  recognizing, 136–139
  and stress response, 136
  water-quality induced, 153–157
Dissolved oxygen, 29
Dominance hierarchies, 51
Domino Damselfish, 61–62
Doryrhamphus
  dactyliophorus, 74
Dragonets, 62–63
Driftwood, 39
Drums, 63
Dry foods, 129, 131
Dwarf Sea Horse, 74

Earthworms, 127
Echinoderms, 97–99
Eclipse Hogfish, 81
Ecsenius
  bicolor, 56
  midas, 56
Elacatinus oceanops, 64–65
Emperor Angelfish, 53
Emperor Snapper, 74
Enteromorpha, 40–41
Ephippidae, 55

Equetus
  acuminatus, 63
  lanceolatus, 63

Fairy Basslets, 54
Fatty acids, 122
Feeding behavior, 120–121
Feeding guidelines,
    131–133
Fiber, 122
Filefishes, 79
Filter materials:
  activated carbon, 17–18
  biomedia rings and
    blocks, 17
  filter floss, 18
Filters, 13
  canister, 16
  cleaning, 117–118
  foam/sponge, 17
  maintenance of, 110
  outside power, 15–16,
    118
  trickle, 15
  undergravel, 14–15, 34,
    117–118
Filtration:
  biological, 9–10
  chemical, 10–11
  mechanical, 10
Fire Goby, 64
Fire Hawkfish, 66
Fish, fresh or frozen, 128
Fish-eye aquarium, 6
Flake foods, 129
Flame Angelfish, 54
Flamefish, 60
Floating thermometer, 20
Flukes, 148
Foam fractionator, 11–12
Food: See also Feeding;
    Nutrition
  dry and freeze-dried,
    129, 131
  fresh and frozen,
    128–129
  live, 125–128
Forcipiger, 57
Forcipiger
  flavissimus, 57
  longirostris, 57
Freckled Hawkfish, 65–66
Freeze-dried foods, 131
French Angelfish, 53
Fresh food, 128–129
Frozen food, 128–129

Fu-Manchu Lionfish, 72
Fungal diseases, 149–150

Giant Jawfish, 66
Glass aquarium, 4–5
Goatfishes, 63–64
Gobiodon okinawae, 64
Golden Blenny, 56
Gold-Striped Cardinalfish,
    60
Gomphosus varius, 81
Gramma
  loreto, 54
  melacara, 54
Green Chromis, 62
Grunts, 65

Haemulidae, 65
Halimeda opuntia, 42–43
Harlequin Bass, 72
Harlequin Pipefish, 74
Hawkfishes, 65–66
Heater, 19–20, 110–111
Heavy metals, 156–157
Heniochus acuminatus, 57
Herbivores, 120–121
Hermit Crabs, 90
High Hat, 63
Hippocampus
  erectus, 74
  reidi, 74
  zosterae, 74
Holocentridae, 75
Humu-Humu, 78
Hydrometer, 30

Invertebrates, 83
  acclimating, 84
  in community aquariums,
    84–85
  feeding guidelines,
    133–134
  purchasing, 84
  species of, 85–99

Jackknife Fish, 63
Jawfishes, 66–67

Koran Angelfish, 53

Labridae, 80–81
Lactoria cornuta, 80
Lemonpeel Angelfish, 54
Leptoscarus vaigiensis, 68
Lighting requirements,
    22–23

bulbs
  and illumination, 224
  replacing, 24, 117
  intensity, 23
  spectra, 23
Lipids, 121–122
Liquid-crystal
    thermometer, 20, 22
Live food, 125–128
Long-Finned Batfish, 55
Long-Horned Cowfish, 80
Longnosed Butterflyfish, 57
Longnosed Filefish, 79
Longnosed Hawkfish, 66
Longsnout Sea Horse, 74
Lutjanidae, 74–75
Lutjanus
  sebae, 74
  spilurus, 74
Lymphocystis, 153
Lyretail Blenny, 56

Macroalgae, 41–43
Maintenance of aquarium:
  daily, 110–112
  journal for, 109–110
  weekly/monthly, 112,
    114–118
Mandarin Fish, 62
Marine aquarium, 3.
    See also individual
    species; Water
  acrylic, 5
  air pumps and diffusers,
    19
  all-glass, 4–5
  carrying capacity of,
    47–48
  cleaning, 116–117
  community, 50–51, 84–85
  cover, 22
  decorating, 35, 37–39
  filtration, 9–11
    equipment for, 13–17
    materials for, 17–18
  heaters, 19–20
  introducing new fish into,
    49–50
  lighting requirements,
    22–24
  maintenance of, 109–118
  monitoring, 106–107
  ozone generators, 12–13
  protein skimmers, 11–12
  quarantine, 139–142, 144
  setting up, 43–45

size of, 5–6
substrate for, 33–34
tank
  location of, 33
  shape, 6
thermometer, 20, 22
ultraviolet sterilizers, 13
weight and placement of,
    6–7
Maroon Clownfish, 61
Metabolism, 120
Meyer's Butterflyfish, 59
Minerals, 123, 125
Miniatus Grouper, 72
Mollusks, 93, 95–97
Moorish Idol, 67
Mullidae, 63, 64
Mulloides martinicus, 64
Mussels, fresh or frozen,
    128
Mycobacteriosis, 151, 153
Myripistis murdjan, 75

Naso lituratus, 76
Naso Tang, 76
Natural seawater, 25–26
Nemateleotris
  decora, 64
  magnifica, 64
Neocirrhitus armatus, 66
Neon Goby, 64–65
Nitrate, 10, 32, 101, 114,
    118, 154–155
Nitrification, 9, 34, 103
Nitrite, 9–10, 31–32, 101,
    154
Nitrogen compounds,
    30–32, 154
Nitrogen cycle, 10, 31,
    102–103
Nudibranchs, 96
Nutrition, 119–120
Nutrition-related diseases,
    157

Ocellated Clownfish, 61
Octopuses, 96–97
Omnivores, 121
One-Spot Foxface, 69–70
Ophioblennius atlanticus,
    56
Opistognathidae, 66–67
Opistognathus
  aurifrons, 66
  rhomaleus, 66
  rosenblati, 66

Orange-Lined Triggerfish, 78
Organics, 11–12, 115
Organophosphates, 142, 144
Ornate Butterflyfish, 59
Ostraciidae, 79–80
Ostracion
cubicus, 80
meleagris, 80
Oxycirrhites typus, 66
Oxymonacanthus
longirostris, 79
Ozone generator, 12–13

*P*alette Tang, 76
Pantherfish, 72
Paracanthurus hepatus, 76
Paracirrhites forsteri, 65–66
Parasitic diseases, 145–149
Parrotfishes, 67–68
Parupeneus multifasciatus, 64
Pellet foods, 131
Penicillus capitatus, 42
Pervagor spilasoma, 79
Pesticides, 157
pH, 28–29, 107, 114–115, 118
Phosphate, 32, 115
Pijama Cardinalfish, 60
Pinnatus Batfish, 55
Pipefishes, 74
Plant materials, 128–129
Platax
pinnatus, 55
teira, 55
Plectorhinchus
chaetodonoides, 65
Polka-Dot Boxfish, 80
Pollutants, 26
Pomacanthidae, 53–54
Pomacanthus
imperator, 53
paru, 53
semicirculatus, 53
Pomacentridae, 60–62
Pomacentrus coelestis, 62
Porcupinefishes, 68
Porkfish, 65
Powder-Blue Tang, 76
Premnas biaculeatus, 61
Proteins, 121

Protein skimmer, 11–12, 111
Pseudanthias
pleurotaenia, 73
tuka, 73
Pseudobalistes fuscus, 78
Pseudochromis
diadema, 55
paccagnellae, 55
porphyreus, 55
Pseudopeneus maculatus, 64
Pterapogon kauderni, 60
Pterois volitans, 70
Pufferfishes, 69
Purple Basslet, 55
Purple Fire Goby, 64
Purple Queen, 73

*Q*uarantine, 139–142, 144
Queen Triggerfish, 78

*R*abbitfishes, 69–70
Raccoon Butterflyfish, 59
Redlip Blenny, 56
Reticulated Puffer, 69
Rhinecanthus aculeatus, 78
Rocks, 37–38
Royal Gramma, 54
Russet Squirrelfish, 75

*S*alinity, 29–30, 118
Sargocentron rubrum, 75
Scallops, fresh or frozen, 128
Scallops (live), 93, 95
Scaridae, 67–68
Scorpaenidae, 70, 72
Scorpionfishes, 70, 72
Scrawled Filefish, 79
Sea Anemones, 87
Sea Basses, 72–73
Sea Cucumbers, 99
Sea Horses, 73–74
Sea Urchins, 98–99
Sebae Clownfish, 61
Selecting fish, 48–49
Serranidae, 72–73
Serranus tigrinis, 72
Shells, 39
Shrimp, fresh or frozen, 128
Shrimp (live), 91–93

Sickness, signs of, 136–139
Siganidae, 69–70
Siganus
unimaculatus, 69–70
virgatus, 70
Skunk Basslet, 55
Small fish (prey food), 127–128
Snails, 95–96
Snappers, 74–75
Sodium chloride, 25
Specific gravity, 29–30
Sphaeramia nematoptera, 60
Sponge Crabs, 91
Spotted Goatfish, 64
Spotted Mandarin, 62
Square Anthias, 73
Squirrelfishes, 75
Starfish, 97–98
Stars-and-Stripes Puffer, 69
Starvation, 157
Stress response, 136
Striped Burrfish, 68
Substrate, 33–35
Surgeonfishes, 75–76
Symphorichthys spilurus, 75
Synchiropus
picturatus, 62
splendidus, 62
Syngnathidae, 73–74
Synthetic seawater, 26–27

*T*ap water, 35
Temperature, 20, 27–28
Territoriality, 51
Tetraodontidae, 69
Thalassoma bifasciatum, 81
Thermometer, 20, 22
Threadfin Butterflyfish, 59
Threadfin Snapper, 75
Three-Striped Damselfish, 62
Toxic gases, 35
Trace elements, 25, 115–116
Triggerfish, 77–79
Trunkfishes, 79–80
Tube Worms, 87–89

Tubifex worms, 127
Twinspot Wrasse, 80–81

*U*dotea
flabellum, 42
spinulosa, 42
Ultraviolet sensor, 13
Undulated Triggerfish, 78

*V*iruses, 153
Vitamins, 122–123
Volitans Lionfish, 70

*W*ater:
changing, 112, 114–116
conditioning period, 26, 35, 101–106
daily check on, 111
dissolved oxygen in, 29
monitoring, 106–107
natural seawater, 25, 26
nitrogen compounds in, 30–32
pH of, 28–29
phosphate in, 32
replacing evaporated, 116
specific gravity and salinity of, 29–30
synthetic seawater, 26–27
temperature require-ments, 20, 27–28
testing, 112, 118
Water-quality induced diseases, 153–157
White spot disease, 146
White worms, 127
Wrasses, 80–81

*Y*ellow Goatfish, 64
Yellow Goby, 64
Yellowhead Jawfish, 66
Yellow Sailfin Tang, 76
Yellow-Tail Wrasse, 81
Yellow Tang, 76

*Z*anclidae, 67
Zanclus canescens, 67
Zebra Lionfish, 70, 72
Zebrasoma
flavescens, 76
veliferum, 76